SPLENDOR AND WONDER
Jesuit Character, Georgetown Spirit, and Liberal Education

SPLENDOR AND WONDER
Jesuit Character, Georgetown Spirit, and Liberal Education

Edited by William J. O'Brien

GEORGETOWN UNIVERSITY PRESS
Washington, D.C.

ISBN 0-87840-477-5
ISBN 0-87840-478-3 (pbk.)

Printed in the United States of America

Library of Congress Cataloging-in-Publication Data

Splendor and wonder: Jesuit character, Georgetown spirit, and liberal education/William J. O'Brien, editor.
p. cm.
Contents: "Splendor and wonder": Ignatian mysticism and the ideals of liberal education/Brian E. Daley—Georgetown's shield, Utraque unum/G. Ronald Murphy—Fat cats or suffering servants?: Georgetown University and the faith that does justice/Walter J. Burghardt—Jesuit education: myth and reality, context and mission/Vincent O'Keefe—The challenge of Georgetown to the Society of Jesus/James A. Devereux—Many worlds and one world: Georgetown and the Society of Jesus in their American context/Leo J. O'Donovan.
ISBN 0-87840-477-5. ISBN 0-87840-478-3 (pbk.)
1. Georgetown University—History. 2. Jesuits—Education—United States—History. 3. Education, Humanistic—United States.
I. O'Brien, William James.
LD1961.G52S65 1988
378.753—dc19 88-24652
CIP

Contents

Preface

The moral commitments upon which our community at Georgetown University is built are rooted in a two-hundred-year commitment to the Ignatian tradition of liberal education. The development of one's personal identity, one's character, takes place within the context of this community through conversation and dialogue, participation and interaction. This context challenges each individual to evaluate judgments and actions in accordance with the ethos of our community. What is required of an individual is more than personal reflection on the implications and consequences of one's actions. It is necessary for each person to see these actions in the context of our ethos and ask: How does my action square with the expectations of this community?

Georgetown University has been providing this context for two hundred years. But a community is constantly changing. Each year, each class of students, each classroom experience, each theater production, each effort to serve others, puts a unique stamp on our community and changes it. It is always necessary to evaluate our ever-changing community in light of the tradition in which Archbishop John Carroll founded our university.

In 1986-1987, the Office of Student Affairs sponsored a series of distinguished lectures that were intended to help clarify for this community the significance of our Ignatian tradition. These lectures offer a powerful statement about the Ignatian spirit at Georgetown.

John J. DeGioia
Dean of Student Affairs

Introduction

The essays which make up this volume represent six attempts to identify that which distinguishes education at Georgetown University. Originally given as Student Affairs distinguished lectures in a series titled "Jesuit Character and Georgetown Spirit," they have been only slightly modified for inclusion here and reflect, therefore, the personalities and styles of their authors. No attempt has been made to effect a uniform style. Although the essays to a greater or lesser extent are rooted in concerns central to Georgetown University, they have relevance wherever the effort is made to comprehend the significance of Jesuit education.

In the opening essay, "Splendor and Wonder: Ignatian Mysticism and the Ideals of Liberal Education," Fr. Brian Daley, S.J., raises a question which is as vexing today as it was when it was first raised centuries ago: "why a Catholic religious order, whose aim is professedly to preach the Gospel of Christ and to carry out the Church's ministry, should be so heavily involved in the troublesome and manifestly secular business of giving young people a general cultural education."

Fr. Daley locates the origin of Jesuit involvement in the business of education in the middle of the sixteenth century, but, rather than trace the history of that involvement, he wonders why it has continued unabated for four centuries. The answer, he thinks, lies in some of the central ideals and goals of the Society: "one must understand something about Jesuit spirituality—. . . the vision of God and the world and human history, and the implications of this vision for the life and prayer of the believer, that is expressed in the key documents of the Society's history, above all in the *Spiritual Exercises* of St. Ignatius."

There follows a brilliant analysis of the *Exercises* in terms of their main elements, moments or stages: wonder, freedom and practical commitment. Each of the elements as elucidated by Fr. Daley sheds light on why Jesuits do what they do. He then goes on to show how the *Constitutions* of the Society of Jesus (written by Ignatius between 1544 and 1556) "envisage the universities of the Society as institutions that will carry on, through academic means, the ministry of evangelization that grew out of the experience of the Exercises." From the beginning, Ignatius included in this academic ministry not only higher studies in theology, but also the humanities, with a view to forming Christian communities "and to prepare young people to strengthen the eloquence of their words, and the sincerity of their faith."

Fr. Daley then displays the complementarity of liberal educational and Jesuit ideals. There is, he says, "an inner affinity between the Christian pedogogy or mystagogy of the *Spiritual Exercises,* that great vehicle for communicating the Jesuit spirit, and the effect on the human person of liberal studies at their best." Both seek "to set up the conditions in which that mind will fall in love with beauty and goodness, will find 'joy in the truth,' so that it might be freed from fear and illusion, might acknowledge the truth for what it is and allow its love of that truth to bear fruit for others."

In his concluding remarks, Fr. Daley acknowledges that, legally, Georgetown is a secular institution, and that its student body and faculty are more clearly pluralistic in their religious and ethical beliefs than in Ignatius's day. Nevertheless, he notes that Jesuits were responsible for the university's foundation and have been centrally involved in its daily life for two centuries; the distinctive goal of Georgetown, and of all its sister institutions, is marked with that Jesuit character rooted in the *Exercises.*

Fr. G. Ronald Murphy, S.J., directs attention to the university's seal to guide reflection on that which distinguishes education at Georgetown. The seal's motto, *Utraque Unum* (Both are One) affords him a title and a theme, one he artfully and engagingly elaborates in the volume's second essay. Attention to the details of the seal and its resemblance to the coat of arms of the United States, the great seal, enables one to get a glimpse of a remarkable feature of Jesuit education.

Fr. Murphy first engages interest in the myth and mystery surrounding the origins of Georgetown's seal. He traces the literary origin of the motto *Utraque Unum* to Ephesians 2:14, the point of which is to tell Christians that, whether they are Gentiles or Jews, they are both one, *utraque unum.* He convincingly suggests that the Georgetown seal is a "commenting allusion" to the motto on the great seal, *E pluribus unum* (From Many, One).

Further attention to the two seals reveals that in the claws of the eagle on Georgetown's seal are not the arrows of war nor the olive branch of peace, but the cross of religion and the globe and calipers of science. Furthermore, above Georgetown's eagle is not a dream of thirteen united colonies, but of a lyre, a harp, a dream of a more ancient harmony. Fr. Murphy sees this attempt "to say something as deeply as it can to the new Republic in the Republic's own language" as characteristically Jesuit, perfectly consistent with Jesuit missionary style.

Fr. Murphy thinks the key to the seal's message is to be discovered in the details of the life of John Carroll, the founder of Georgetown University. Although born in Upper Marlboro, John Carroll at the age of thirteen was sent to Flanders for his education. During his years in Europe, the Catholic religion was suppressed and religious liberty denied. Upon his return to these shores, he "fell totally in love with the American solution to the problem of religion and politics." His proposal for Georgetown University was in harmony with American principles based on the Enlightenment and open to every religion. At the same time it was to be a Roman Catholic institution, *utraque unum.* What a difference from later Catholic colleges and universities established by later immigrants with a view to protecting Catholics from inculturation: "this later development emphasizes all the more Georgetown's unique origin."

The openness to Enlightenment ideals to which Fr. Murphy calls attention is rooted in the same Ignatian spirituality Fr. Daley displays so cogently in his essay. "St. Ignatius insisted that a spiritual person must realize that God dwells in all things and that he can be found in all things—in the stones, in the earth, in the plants and in the sea, and in oneself."

In "Fat Cats or Suffering Servants," Fr. Walter Burghardt, S.J., assumes in turn the roles of observer, theologian and prophet to delineate the dominant culture and the Christian counterculture. He cites first the claims of sociologists that "America's brightest young people are interested more than ever primarily in making money." But if the dominant culture is to be understood in materialistic terms, there is a significant counterculture described by Andrew Greeley which is made up of students like some of those at Georgetown who reach out to the elderly, the underprivileged, the homeless, the young, the delinquent, the immigrant, and the handicapped. The roots of the counterculture Fr. Burghardt locates in the social teaching of the Catholic Church, especially since the Second

Vatican Council. He adds that that social teaching is hardly without precedent: it is itself rooted in the Hebrew and Christian Scriptures.

Finally, Fr. Burghardt plays the prophet and asks whether the counterculture holds a future for his audience. He reminds them that their responsibilities will only become more complex upon graduation and could prevent them from living out the vision of the counterculture. Yet his hopes remain high, that "however radical the risk, however many the Judases who betray you, even on your cross you will always be Christ the lover, arms extended to your little world for its redemption—and yours."

Fr. Vincent O'Keefe, S.J., moves from a humorous commentary on the myth or common perception of Jesuit education to a consideration of its reality. With Fr. Daley, he locates the source of authentic Jesuit spirit in the *Exercises,* from which one can learn one's origin and nature as well as one's end and the end of human society. Characteristic of Jesuit education is a "concern to develop intellectual probity, a critical intelligence, and a responsible freedom." At the same time, Fr. O'Keefe emphasizes that "the Jesuit spirit and heritage is rooted in the Church's tradition," which "looks to all cultures and races, and to all areas of human concern." An understanding of the relation of the university to the church from the beginning of that relationship helps one to understand appropriately the context of Jesuit higher education. Attention to more recent papal statements suggests a particular mission for the Jesuit educator: an apostolate to the culture of the surrounding world, a Christian penetration of that world.

Fr. James Devereux, S.J., shifts the focus from the significance of the Jesuit tradition for Georgetown to the challenge which Georgetown University offers the Society of Jesus: the challenge is a tension between opportunities and obstacles. Fr. Devereux sharply distinguishes between the university as a secular institution and the Society of Jesus as a religious community, though he finds in them many aspirations in common. In answer to the question, "how can they [Jesuits] contribute to the life of this institution in a way that is consonant with the community's own purposes?" Fr. Devereux recalls the words of King Lear: "Who is it that can tell me who I am?" Indeed, he suggests, the Jesuits can offer Georgetown University its identity, a precious, life-giving gift. Accordingly, in the university's current prospectus, one reads "Georgetown, by virtue of its Catholic and Jesuit origins, has a rich and special view of reality, one that celebrates human dignity in a godly context." If anything, Jesuit education is about the synthesis of Christianity and human culture.

There are other ways the Society of Jesus offers Georgetown an identity, as when Fr. Healy "proposed to the faculty the characteristically Ignatian synthesis of contemplation and action as a pattern for the life of the University." Furthermore, the Society of Jesus offers members of the university community a method: the *Spiritual Exercises* of St. Ignatius.

In all of these remarks, Fr. Devereux describes the opportunities which Georgetown University affords the Society of Jesus. But part of Georgetown's challenge is rooted in the obstacles which confront the Society, not the least of which is declining numbers of Jesuits. There do not need to be many Jesuits at Georgetown, but there need to be some. Another obstacle to the Society of Jesus is, ironically, the fact that the university has become a fashionable place to be, all too in tune with "the values of contemporary American culture, some of which stand in direct contradiction to Christianity." Finally, Fr. Devereux points out that many on the faculty simply do not share the vision of education articulated in the prospectus and other university documents. Nevertheless, despite the obstacles, the Society of Jesus "commits itself to the life of this place of Catholic learning, and in so doing renews its own life."

In this volume's concluding essay, Fr. Leo O'Donovan, S.J., attempts to explain how Georgetown University can on the one hand be very particular and on the other hand have universal concerns. From its beginning, Georgetown has been open to students of every religious persuasion. Furthermore, there exists a multiplicity of cultures which shape very different ways of being in the world, both for the American and for the Catholic. In short, Georgetown "has many worlds to meet." The challenge to respond to King Lear's question is great indeed. There is, however, a way. The way to the other's world must be through the particularities of one's own world, particularities which have been critically scrutinized before being accepted. The way to the other's world implies a recognition of the movement, the unfinished character of one's own world, as well as an openness to the other's and a willingness to enter into dialogue with the other in hopes that "a common experience of a common world will arise."

In reflecting on the particularities of this world, Fr. O'Donovan notes that both as Americans and as Catholics we face changes more rapid that we can understand or control. Nonetheless, he believes that we are more religious than we have recently been encouraged to believe and are deeply interested in issues of justice and peace. He sees the university as a "place of education for a world, the preparation of citizens, the cultivation of men and women who may become . . . 'planetary people'," knowing all the while that "not from any of our own works but only from the cross of Jesus Christ do we really have hope for God's true world to come."

This volume of essays which has sought to capture the Ignatian spirit at the heart of Georgetown University was the work of many hands. It is my pleasure to acknowledge those who have in different ways made this volume possible: Verona Kelly, Mary Jean DeCrane, Mary Gerity, Wendy Felker, Tracy Preston, and Cynthia McMullen, who helped to prepare the talks for publication; John Breslin, S.J., and Eleanor Waters of the Georgetown University Press, who patiently edited the text; and most especially, the Jesuit Community at Georgetown University, which has chosen to make this volume of essays its gift to the university on the occasion of its bicentennial.

William J. O'Brien
Assistant to the Dean of Student Affairs

Brian E. Daley, S.J.

"Splendor and Wonder": Ignatian Mysticism and the Ideals of Liberal Education

Brian E. Daley, S.J., is Associate Professor of Historical Theology at the Weston School of Theology.

I

In the year 1605, the Spanish Jesuit Pedro de Ribadeneyra published a bulky volume entitled *A Treatise Explaining the Religious Institution of the Society of Jesus.*[1] Almost eighty years old by then, Fr. Ribadeneyra knew the Society, and the story of its origins, perhaps better than anyone else alive. He had been one of the first novices admitted by Ignatius Loyola, after the Society had received papal approval as a religious institute in 1540; he had known Ignatius intimately, until the founder's death in 1556, and had spent much of his life after that trying to explain Jesuit ideals and Jesuit ways to his contemporaries. This book was published privately, for Jesuit consumption only, and seems to have been known in Spain by the short title *El Porqué*—"The Why and the Wherefore"—since it was meant to explain to Ribadeneyra's younger brethren, to Jesuits of the third and fourth generation, why the Society had developed some of the peculiar practices for which it was known and criticized. Chapter 39 of the treatise[2] is entitled, "Why the Society Teaches Boys Grammar," and deals with a question that was apparently as vexing to Jesuits and their friends at the turn of the seventeenth century as it is today: why a Catholic religious order, whose aim is professedly to preach the gospel of Christ and to carry out the church's ministry, should be so heavily involved in the troublesome and manifestly secular business of giving young people a general cultural education.

People criticize the Jesuit practice of teaching the humanities, Ribadeneyra writes, for several reasons. No other religious order, they say, runs schools;[3] such a responsibility seems to contradict the seriousness, the *gravitas,* of a religious community.[4] Further, people argue, "it is a repulsive, annoying and burdensome thing to guide and teach and try to control a crowd of young people, who are naturally so frivolous, so restless, so talkative and so unwilling to work that even their parents cannot keep them at home. So it happens that our young Jesuits, who are involved in teaching them, lead a very strained life, wear down their energies and damage their health."[5] Many young Jesuits, he adds, who are talented enough to achieve something substantial in academic research, "are prevented from doing so because they are occupied by these childish and inconsequential trifles."[6] In reply, Fr. Ribadeneyra is willing to concede that teaching *is* hard work, and may even be damaging to the health—though he asks his readers rather pointedly whether they think preaching and hearing confessions and doing the other typical Jesuit ministries are exactly "a recreation for body and spirit."[7] But he argues, in defense of the Society's practice of running schools, that the education of youth in the traditional values of their culture is the foundation of any well-governed republic,[8] and a work long blessed by the documents and tradition of the church. The history of Christian institutions abounds, he assures his readers, in attempts by holy people to provide for the young an education that is respectable by both secular and religious standards.[9] More important, he argues, the strongest influence on the development of moral character in a young person is "the life of the teacher: the holier and more perfect he is, the more easily and powerfully he will imprint on the tender souls of the young the form of virtue and the love of an upright life"[10]—qualities sorely needed in those worst of times![11] To be an early and lasting influence on character, he concludes, is "what the Society is seeking through this most laborious of its ministries. I do not know whether there is any other work in which it more fully reveals its service of the Divine Majesty than in the literary education of adolescents."[12]

"Its service of the Divine Majesty": in using this solemn phrase so dear to Ignatius Loyola, Ribadeneyra clearly wanted to underscore the connection he saw between the work of basic cultural education and the deepest ideals and longings of the Society of Jesus. It was not, after all, obvious. The Jesuits had moved into the business of education very early in their history, but more or less by accident. As university graduates themselves, Ignatius and his first companions agreed it was important that the young men who wished to join them should also receive the best education available, not only in theology and scriptural languages, but in literature, logic, mathematics, philosophy and the natural sciences. Classical literary studies, as Ignatius' secretary Juan Polanco once assured his more skeptical confrere Diego Laynez, both prepare the young Jesuits' minds for theology and lead, even by themselves, to "the greater service of God and the help of our neighbor."[13] The contribution of the Society to this educational enterprise, however, during its first few years, was simply to establish residences—*collegia*—for its own student members in the great university cities of Europe. But the rapid growth in the number of aspiring candidates soon made it necessary to open colleges for young Jesuits in smaller provincial cities, where there were no universities, and so to staff them with Jesuit teachers and administrators. That step led to a fateful chain of consequences. First—as at Gandia in Spain in 1546—other students urgently asked to join the Jesuit scholastics in their courses. Then, in 1547, the city fathers of Messina in Sicily succeeded in persuading Ignatius to found a college there, not for young Jesuits but simply for the boys of the town: an institution combining what we would think of today as both secondary and undergraduate higher education. Before long, every bishop, city council and Catholic prince of Europe was pestering the Jesuits to open another college or to found even a new university in their back yard, and the long tradition of Jesuit education was under way.

My purpose here is not to chart the course of that tradition, much less to situate the history of Georgetown University within it. It is rather to reflect again on the question that Ribadeneyra tried to answer for his own time: if involvement in humanistic or liberal education began, for Jesuits, by an accident of history, why has that involvement continued unabated for more than four centuries? How can one make sense—for Jesuits and their friends, as well as for the wider public—of the commitment of this body of Catholic priests and their clerical associates to an enterprise that is not, in itself, explicitly religious at all, and that necessarily occupies itself much of the time with purely secular pursuits? What I want to argue is that the continuing connection between Jesuits and humanistic or liberal studies is not fortuitous; that Jesuits have remained in this work throughout their history because it realizes, in a subtle yet profound way, some of the central ideals and goals of the Society; and that the value of liberal education as a Jesuit priestly ministry—the reason ministers of the gospel would even consider teaching unruly boys Latin literature, or unruly modern undergraduates a host of other things—lies, for the Jesuit spirit, not simply in the possible personal influence of the teacher on his pupils, as Ribadeneyra argued, but in the very content of the educational enterprise, in the work itself.

II

To understand the point I am trying to make, one must understand something about Jesuit spirituality—about what I have called here, perhaps rather flamboyantly, "Jesuit mysticism": the vision of God and the world and human history, and the implications of this vision for the life and prayer of the believer, that is expressed in the key documents of the Society's history, above all in the *Spiritual Exercises* of St. Ignatius.[14] As anyone knows who has tried to use it, the book called the *Spiritual Exercises* is not meant for the casual or the devotional reader. It is a plan, an instruction manual rather than a treatise on spiritual theology. It is a guide for a director trying to help a fellow Christian through several days—or better yet, several weeks—of intense and highly structured prayer, reflection and self-examination, in the hope of experiencing for himself or herself the same conversion to Christian discipleship, the same powerful focusing of commitment to the Lord and union with him, that Ignatius experienced at the turning point of his own life of faith.

In the first "week" or phase of the *Exercises,* the subject is asked to deepen his awareness of himself before God as the Christian faith understands each of us to be: a graced sinner, an unloving creature who is much loved by his creator, the receiver of a gift who tends to forget the giver and regard the gift as his own. So the meditations suggested for the first "week" of the *Exercises* move back and forth among the themes of creation, sin and forgiveness, in the context of one's own personal history: not in order to force from the exercitant an artificial sense of guilt, but to elicit a "cry of wonder" at the full implications of Jesus' word that "our sins are forgiven."[15] It is an attempt to move the exercitant gently toward a deeper vision of the truth about himself, as the Christian faith proclaims that truth, so that the truth can genuinely make him free from both illusion and anxiety.

In the second "week" or phase of the *Exercises,* the subject is urged to move on in this freedom, into the fullness of Christian discipleship. The focus now is not on ourselves but on Jesus, as the one in whom God's saving involvement in our history has taken human shape. Ignatius leads the exercitant, in the second "week," to contemplate the whole career of Jesus in loving detail: the plan of God to make the world his kingdom through the message of Jesus; God's providential decision to send his Son into the world as a human being; the birth and childhood, preaching and miracles of the Lord. And as the pattern unfolds, the exercitant is asked to keep inserting himself or herself into the picture: asked repeatedly whether he or she is willing to let Jesus' form of life, not only as a program for action but as a state of mind and heart, become his own. The goal of this second "week" is clearly, as I have said, a kind of conversion, a commitment of the exercitant's whole person and energies to following Jesus on his way of self-effacing service and sonship. And the exercitant is urged to let this commitment, in his or her own prayerful reflection, take on the most concrete form possible: to let it become the driving force behind a reordering of his or her priorities and a reshaping of the details of his or her daily occupations.

The flavor of contemplative prayer in this second week, then, is, on the one hand, thoroughly practical. Yet it leads inevitably in the direction of a kind of mystical union, as well: of an identification of the exercitant with Jesus that goes beyond imitation and admiration, goes beyond even the categories of thought and imagination, and that is explicable only in terms of love.[16] The rest of the *Exercises* is aimed at deepening this union of disciple and master by drawing the exercitant into the passage of Jesus through death to life that we call the "Paschal Mystery." In the third "week" or phase, the exercitant contemplates, step by step, Jesus' passion and death; in the fourth "week," his appearances to his disciples as risen Lord, his sending of the Holy Spirit at Pentecost, and his empowering the disciples to found a church. The goal in these final two "weeks" is not to provoke a new conversion, or to move the exercitant to add details to the decisions he or she has already made. It is simply to allow his or her identification with the Lord to grow and become anchored in the central mystery of Christian faith, the death and resurrection of Jesus. Later in his career, Ignatius tells us, he prayed earnestly to God that God would "place" him with his Son, Jesus; this placement, this situation of the believer with Jesus is really the goal of the whole *Exercises,* as I understand them, the bridge between the mystical prayer of union with Jesus and the practical Christian involvement in the world that is the distinctive mark of Jesuit spirituality.

Three main elements, I think, three "moments" or stages, characterize the whole direction of the exercitant's prayer and inner affections during the four "weeks" I have just briefly described. The first element is a loving wonder at the goodness and mercy of God: a wonder called forth by our contemplation of the world around us and of the human history we live in. In the first "week" of the *Exercises* especially, but throughout their whole process, Ignatius invites the exercitant to contemplate all of reality in the context of God's creation and redemption, in order to respond spontaneously with thanks and praise, to be moved to engage oneself in this world, in this history, as a willing response of love. Ignatian contemplation is not abstract reasoning about God, nor is it the kind of contemplation that seeks to leave words and images behind, in order to enter the "cloud of unknowing." Rather, it is a contemplative prayer that gazes in faith at creation; it turns in faith, again and again, to look at the world and to find God's presence in it, because it knows that the world itself, when seen in faith, is enough to move the heart to the active love of God.

The second movement that the *Exercises* hope to elicit is growth in freedom through a deeper personalization of the truth about God and ourselves. The *Exercises* are designed to be a training in freedom: not freedom in the empty, formal sense of a simple lack of restraints, but freedom from the fear and ignorance that lie at the root of most of our self-seeking, freedom to be ourselves as God sees us—creatures who are dependent yet self-determining, sinners who are loved and forgiven—and freedom to act in that self-awareness without the need to secure or deceive ourselves. Ignatian spirituality, like the structures of the Society of Jesus that it inspired, is a spirituality based on freedom in the Lord—a freedom to follow the call of Christian discipleship as one hears it, limited only by the responsibility implied in the call itself: the responsibility to obey God and his ecclesial representatives in a spirit of faith and love.

The third element in the spiritual movement of the *Exercises* grows out of these first two: a commitment to action in the world, a concern not to let the conversion one has undergone remain a mere surge of feelings or a change in ideas, but to let it become the basis of a new, carefully planned way of life as a Christian disciple. In a key contemplation of the fourth "week," often used as the final reflection of all—the exercise Ignatius calls "A Contemplation for Obtaining Love"—the exercitant is asked to take a long, global view of all creatures, from the perspective of his own place in creation and his own history, and to see in all creatures an overwhelming proof of God's personal, provident love for him. Presupposing, as he says, that genuine love "shows itself in deeds rather than in words," and that it leads to giving, to sharing what one has with the beloved,[17] Ignatius asks the exercitant to let the love that has touched and freed him throughout the *Exercises* move him now to give himself away in faith-filled action—to return to the God who so loves me "all that I have and possess,"[18] in the full concreteness of my own history. Here, as always, Ignatian mysticism is a mysticism realized in loving union, but a mysticism oriented to practice.

These three elements that characterize the movement of the *Spiritual Exercises*—wonder, freedom and practical commitment—are expressed, perhaps, more simply and more clearly still at the very start of the process, in the preliminary consideration Ignatius calls the "First Principle and

Foundation," the presupposition, for what is to follow. "We are created," he asserts, "to praise, reverence and serve God our Lord, and by this means to save our souls."[19] The reason for our being, as limited realities who depend on absolute reality, is that we might be caught up in wonder at reality and praise its source; that we might realize the truth about ourselves and our fellow creatures and be freed by that truth to act with the reverence, the recognition of value, that gives our freedom content and meaning; and that we might serve God our Lord in the midst of his creatures, realize our praise and reverence in other-centered action, freely give ourselves to God and each other in love. "To praise, reverence and serve God our Lord" as a creature among creatures, and "by this means" to realize and fulfill what we are made to be, to "save our souls": such a description of the purpose of our lives is, for Ignatius, the "principle and foundation" not only of these four "weeks" of prayer but of all Christian growth and conversion, and the basis of Christian action. To let it become the orienting principle of one's life is the real purpose of the *Spiritual Exercises.*

III

We have been considering the Ignatian *Exercises* and their brand of practical mysticism not simply as a phenomenon in the history of Christian faith, but because of the light they shed on why Jesuits do what they do. The *Constitutions* of the Society of Jesus, the description of its life and ideals that Ignatius painstakingly wrote and rewrote between 1544 and his death in 1556,[20] makes that fairly clear: the purpose of the organization, in the eyes of its original members, was to be an instrument of active, up-to-date pastoral ministry within the Catholic Church, exercised by those who had been "converted" to discipleship as Ignatius had been. As they wandered through the towns of northern Italy in the early 1540s, preaching, hearing confessions, giving popular lectures on the faith, and caring for the poor, the first Jesuits came to be known as "reformed priests": priests whose life and ministry had been shaped by thorough academic training, and reshaped by the spiritual transformation of the *Exercises,* to meet the needs of a church crying out for structural and practical renewal. The work of these early Jesuits could be classified chiefly as a ministry of the *word:* a ministry of instruction aimed at groups and individuals, children and adults, the educated and the ignorant, which had as its purpose and content the proclamation and explanation of the Christian gospel.

As the Society found itself involved in running academic institutions, in founding first colleges and then full-scale universities, it naturally regarded this work, too, as an extension of preaching, a part of its ministry of the word. Universities in the sixteenth century were, in general, still organized according to the medieval model; they consisted of an undergraduate faculty of arts, and usually of the three graduate or professional faculties of law, medicine, and theology. Naturally enough, the Jesuits made use of this model, but in a self-consciously selective way. So Ignatius writes in the fourth part of the *Constitutions:* "Since the end of the Society and of its studies is to aid our fellow men and women to the knowledge and love of God and the salvation of their souls, and since the branch of theology is the means most suitable to this end, in the universities of the Society the principal emphasis ought to be put upon it."[21]

The first Jesuit universities, in other words, saw themselves first of all as faculties of theology, professional training centers for those preparing themselves to join in the Jesuit work of an intellectually and spiritually "reformed" priesthood. "Moreover," Ignatius continues, "since both the learning of theology and the use of it require (especially in these times) knowledge of humane letters"—by which, as he explains in a note, he means literature, rhetoric and history—"and of the Latin, Greek and Hebrew languages, there should be capable professors of these languages, and that in sufficient number."[22] "Likewise, since the arts or natural sciences"—in which he includes the various branches of philosophy and mathematics—"dispose the intellectual powers for theology and are useful for the perfect understanding and use of it, and also by their own nature help towards the same ends"—the knowledge and love of God—"they should be treated with fitting diligence and by learned professors. In all this the honor and glory of God our Lord should be sincerely sought."[23] Medicine and law, however, "being more remote from our Institute," will either not be taught in Jesuit universities at all, or will be taught by laymen.[24]

The *Constitutions,* in other words, envisage the universities of the Society as institutions that will carry on, through academic means, the ministry of evangelization that grew out of the experience of the *Exercises* and was the reason for the Society's existence: helping people to know and love God for themselves, giving God honor and glory by leading his creatures to a loving faith. The fact that Ignatius includes in this academic ministry not only higher studies in theology—formal thinking about God and his mysteries—but also the humanities, the general range of cultural subjects then taught to young people in their early and middle teens—Latin and Greek, poetry and rhetoric, mathematics and ethics and the natural sciences—is clearly of enormous importance for the later history of the Jesuit order and its institutions. But how does Ignatius come to see such subjects as belonging to the proper work of his "reformed priests"? How does he integrate the liberal arts into a ministry of the word?

One way, clearly, in which Ignatius thought the teaching of the humanities would work an evangelical purpose was through the unambiguously Catholic character of the new Jesuit colleges, and the purposefully Christian style and method of teaching that was to be employed.[25] The Jesuits' approach to the work of education was meant, from the start, to be distinctive. Following the instructional system of the University of Paris rather than the more impersonal model of the Italian universities, Ignatius directed that teaching in the universities of the Society should combine a few large-scale, formal lectures with frequent regular sessions in small groups, for discussion and clarification, in a highly complicated and tightly organized pattern. The level of instruction was to be carefully adjusted to the tested capabilities of the student—a feature that was apparently lacking in other universities of the age. Collaboration was to be another trademark: members of Jesuit faculties were instructed to work together, even to hold carefully umpired public disputations (the sixteenth century's version of team-teaching!), while the more advanced students were also to be involved in teaching their younger peers.[26] A prime emphasis was to be on teaching the art of expression, the use of the word;[27] on the other hand, little outward stress was to be placed on ceremony, titles or degrees, either among the senior students or among the faculty.[28] Most important of all, perhaps—at least for us who labor in modern American academia—all teaching in Jesuit universities was to be free of charge, "for according to our Institute, our reward should be only Christ our Lord, who is 'our reward exceeding great'."[29]

Students of all ages in the early Jesuit colleges were expected, too, to learn Catholic doctrine as a central part of their academic program, and to participate in a highly organized pattern of liturgical and devotional practice—one not very different from that prescribed for the young members of the Society. Boys in the college at Messina—who probably ranged in age from ten to eighteen or nineteen—were taught catechism every Friday and heard a lecture on some religious subject every Sunday and holyday.[30] Each class day was to begin and end with a period of prayer,[31] and all the students were to be taught how to pray, verbally and mentally, and how to examine their consciences.[32] They attended daily Mass, were expected to confess at least once a month, and were urged to spend at least some time in prayer on rising and on going to bed.[33] Ignatius insisted that no one be forced to attend religious services against his will; the reluctant "should be persuaded gently, and not be forced to it, nor expelled from the schools for not complying."[34] Even so, the Jesuit founders seem to have assumed that their lay pupils would gradually become people whose lives were rooted in prayer; so the *Constitutions* of the College at Messina lay down—astonishingly, perhaps, to us in a more secular age—that each student, before making any important life decision, should "pray diligently, with great devotion and with full readiness to deny his own will."[35] Likewise, sober and responsible Christian behavior was expected of all. Games were severely restricted,[36] and the students were taught to keep strict account of their use of time;[37] swearing, using vulgar language and the carrying of weapons were forbidden.[38]

The structure of Jesuit educational institutions that begins to emerge in the *Constitutions,* and that is reinforced in the letters and documents issued by Jesuit educators during the next half-century, is a curious combination of sophistication and evangelical simplicity. Education was to be carefully planned, organized down to the last proseminar, and uniformly realized through all the Society's provinces—it was really the first educational *system* of the modern world. The best contemporary methods were to be used, the most up-to-date and comprehensive books to be read; yet the purpose of the system, in the end, was to form schools that were Christian communities, and to prepare young people to strengthen and reform the wider Christian community by the clarity of their thinking, the eloquence of their words, and the sincerity of their faith.

Closely connected with these structural features, in Ignatius' view, was the personal aspect of education as a ministry: the heart of the system, the key to its evangelistic effectiveness, was to be the behavior of the teachers themselves. It was they, personally, in their attitudes and in the clarity of their intention, who had to make their work in the classroom, whether drilling Greek conjugations or explaining the refinements of Aristotelian metaphysics, into a ministry of the word, an echo of their Ignatian wonder at creation. "The teachers," Ignatius directs, "should make it their special aim, both in their lectures when occasion is offered and outside them, too, to inspire the students to the love and service of God our Lord, and to a love of the virtues by which they will please him. They should urge the students to direct all their studies to this end."[39]

The structure, then, and the manner—the distinctive style and system—of early Jesuit education were surely conceived as important ways in which the apparently secular academic enterprise was to be integrated into the Society's ministerial purpose, seen as a legitimate brand of Christian and priestly service. And yet I think there was more—I think, as I have already mentioned, that the reason early Jesuits found teaching the humanities a congenial way to exercise their ministry goes even beyond the personal and institutional aspects, the "how" of education, to include its content: the "what," the matter of liberal studies itself. Let me explain.

IV

"Liberal" education is, etymologically, the kind of education suitable for a free citizen, the primary training desirable for a person who will be engaged in, and in some degree responsible for, the body politic. In ancient Greece and Rome, it was primarily training in the use of language: training for effectiveness in expression, for an understanding of the literature that shapes and hands on a culture, for skill in the rules of argument and the arts of persuasion. The goal of such education was to form, in Cicero's phrase, "a person of perfect eloquence,"[40] a person who knew the right way to say anything at all and who was not afraid to put that competence to work. At its worst, Greek and Roman education produced pedants, dilettantes and lawyers; at its best, it produced the citizens of relatively stable and relatively democratic societies.

In our own culture, "liberal" education means general education, education in values, education for wisdom rather than for marketability: not specialized training in the skills and information one needs for a career, but a process whereby one comes to know more fully the accomplishments and ideals of one's culture, in order to evaluate and redirect one's personal accomplishments and ideals.

The goal of this general education, however one wants to define its content, is surely to work a kind of inner transformation: to stimulate a young mind to wonder at the world's beauty, to excitement at its complexity, to compassion at its vulnerability; to make that mind more deeply and reflectively aware of the ideals and values it is offered by its forebears, and to encourage a person, at the most adaptable and idealistic time of his life, to sift and organize those ideals for himself and commit himself fearlessly to what he sees to be good. That is why liberal or humanistic education is usually so preoccupied with the past: with history and the classics of literature, with monuments of art and great works in philosophy and important milestones in the growth of science. It is not because these things are old that they are worth studying, but because they have made us what we are, because they express so typically, so classically, the things that human experience has found true and worth knowing. The first purpose of liberal education, surely, is to induce delight and amazement, as well as tempered sorrow, at what humanity has discovered and done; it is to lead us to that "joy in the truth" that St. Augustine identifies as the root of faith, the paradigm for all our knowledge and love of God.[41]

The general, value-centered character of this kind of education, too, is why we call it "liberal": why we see it as essentially suited to free people, people responsible for their own destiny, rather than for slaves. In the ancient world, such a general course of studies was something that only a free citizen, a citizen who someday would have voice and vote in the public councils and who might even run for public office, would find useful. It was also something that only a free citizen was likely to have the leisure and the money to afford. But then and now, I think it has also been assumed that contact with truth and beauty is not only exciting but liberating in itself: that the truth *does* make us free to be ourselves and to engage the world realistically and fruitfully. And this liberating effect of the truth is why its purveyors generally insist so passionately on the freedom of teachers and students to search for it without prior political or ideological restraint. Academic freedom, surely, is anything but academic irresponsibility—the freedom to use the ivy-mantled walls as a safe place to fire off one's favorite ideas, without regard for their public effect. It is rather the freedom, in Paul's phrase, to "speak the truth in love," as best one can. Only love, only respect and concern for the welfare of others, makes what we speak in freedom *true* in its full sense. And only when we are free to acknowledge and to love the truth for its own sake, to cherish what is beautiful because it is beautiful and do the good because it is good—only then is the human spirit in the position to look beyond self-preservation and acknowledge the reality of other beings (and of ultimate being, which we call God) as valuable and lovable in their own right. Only in a context of freedom, to use Ignatian terms, is the human spirit able to move from praise to reverence, from "joy in the truth" to the acknowledgment that that truth is at least as valuable as I am, and may not be manipulated or subordinated to my self-interest. And only in a spirit of reverence for the truth and for the value of others does freedom, academic or otherwise, become a human and a social good.

The value-centered character of what we call liberal education, finally, is also the best explanation of its practical importance. From Plato to John Dewey, philosophers of education have insisted that the ultimate purpose of studying language and literature and the best products of human thought is a moral and social one: to equip a free citizen to take an active and intelligent part in the life of his or her city, and to work for its good. For this reason, educators in the classical tradition have insisted that a student's brush with the humanities involve not merely the acquisition of the technical skills of persuasion and argument, but the formation of character, the refinement and deepening of moral ideals, through hard thinking and through conversation with wise and good people, in order to insure that the trained persuader not be a menace to society. Quintilian, the first-century Roman professor of rhetoric, sums up this concern well in the preface to his influential rhetorical textbook: "Our aim," he says, "has been to educate the perfect orator, who is none other than the good man. Therefore we demand of him not only outstanding ability in public speaking, but all the virtues of the human spirit. I do not agree that the principles of upright and decent living should be made—as some think—the province of philosophy, since the truly civic-minded man—the one who is suited to be a leader in both public and private affairs, who can rule cities with his advice, found them with his legislation and reform them with his judgments—is, in the end, no other than the orator."[42]

The education of the verbally skillful citizen, in this classical view, is nothing less than a training for political leadership. For this reason, if such education is to do society good, it has to involve a kind of conversion—a conversion philosophical, if not religious, in nature: an awakening and a focusing of human ideals and desires in a young person's mind that will drive him to change the pattern of his life, and then to commit his energies to realizing those ideals concretely in a social as well as a personal way. Like the philosopher described in Plato's *Republic,* a person freed from illusion and ignorance by a careful program of mental discipline has rightly been expected, in our Western culture, to return to the cave of shadows and to work selflessly there for the liberation of the other prisoners who were once his fellows.

V

The general description I have been giving of what we mean by "liberal" education is, of course, open to dispute, and in need of much further nuance and application. My purpose here is not to develop a new philosophy of education, or to revive older ones, but simply to summarize a classical view of education (and one, I admit, that I believe in) in order to explain why I think Jesuits have been drawn, since their earliest days, into teaching the humanities as a part of their effort to communicate the Christian gospel: why they have not only run seminaries and schools of theology like the one I work in, but have been involved in the very secular business of teaching grammar and rhetoric, sociology and linguistics, even of fund-raising and administration and trusteeship, from the days of the old Roman College to these days of Georgetown University. The reason, as I have said before, seems not simply to be that Jesuit schools respect Christian and personal values, or that teaching of any sort allows the teacher to exercise a moral influence on his pupils. These things are, of course, true. But there is, in addition, I think, a deep correspondence, an inner affinity, between the Christian pedagogy or mystagogy of the *Spiritual Exercises,* that great vehicle for communicating the Jesuit spirit, and the effect on the human person of liberal studies at their best. Both are centered, in their own way, on rhetoric: on the laborious process of training the human mind to understand the truth and to speak it powerfully. Both seek, more importantly, to lead the human mind from praise to reverence to service: to set up the conditions in which that mind will fall in love with beauty and goodness, will find "joy in the truth," so that it might be freed from fear and illusion, might acknowledge the truth for what it is and allow its love of that truth to bear fruit for others. Wonder at the world, liberation from enclosure in the self, and commitment to service: these traditional goals of classical education became, for Ignatius and his followers—all children of the Renaissance—implicitly, if not consciously, the main way-stations in the spiritual education of the *Exercises,* and allowed them to find in the enterprise of humanistic training for eloquence not only a beneficial secular tradition but a parallel to their main work, a promising prospect for a new and thoroughly Christian ministry.

"They should often be exhorted," Ignatius wrote of young Jesuits beginning their training, "to seek God our Lord in all things, stripping off from themselves the love of creatures, to the extent this is possible, in order to turn their love upon the Creator of them, by loving him in all creatures and all of them in him . . . "[43] This same mystical ideal was to be the goal in teaching lay students, as well, in the first public Jesuit college at Messina: "All shall keep reverence for God before the eyes of their mind," states the founding charter of the school, "and embrace it with all their heart . . . Let all make the honor and glory of God the end not only of their studies but of all their activities."[44] Liberal education seems to have been, in the eyes of the early Jesuits, an unusually promising means to help young people learn to find God in all things, simply because creation itself—the object contemplated so globally by liberal education—was, for Jesuit mysticism, resplendent with God's glory and radiant with his love.

American colleges and universities today that stand in the Jesuit tradition—institutions like Georgetown—are, of course, a very different kind of institution from the college at Messina. Academically, they are vastly larger and more ambitious undertakings. Legally, they are secular institutions, owned and guided not by the Society of Jesus or by the Catholic hierarchy, but by independent boards of trustees. Both the student body and the faculty, at Georgetown and in every Jesuit college today, are more clearly pluralistic in their religious and ethical beliefs than would have been conceivable in Ignatius' day; while the student body at Georgetown has never been exclusively Catholic, and sometimes was not even predominantly so, plurality of background and of religious allegiance is something we not only tolerate today, but something we celebrate. As a result, it is no longer so obvious to the members of a varied community such as this that the purpose of our humanistic studies is to learn to find God in all things, and to work for his glory.

Yet it is important for all who study and teach, as we like to say, "in the Jesuit tradition," to recognize that what we do here has been conceived by the representatives of that tradition since its origins as part of a greater mystical and moral enterprise: part of the chance given each of us, part of the duty incumbent on each of us, as creatures, to search for "the unknown God," to strive to hear his word and keep it, to struggle to find his love in the world that we accept as his gift, and to love him and all his creatures totally in return. Our words, our notions for this enterprise will surely differ, but Georgetown's historic purpose has been to draw us all, in one way or another, to engage in it.

We are searching, in this series of talks—as its title suggests—for connections between those two elusive entities we call "the Jesuit character" and "the Georgetown spirit." We do this because we recognize that it is in our history, our origins, as well as in our hopes and desires for our future, that we discover what we really are. Georgetown's curriculum, our conception of what makes good teaching and good learning, our sense of priorities for campus life and of the importance of campus ministry, our hopes for how Georgetown graduates will live and what they will do—surely the distinctive flavor of all these things is determined not simply by location or historical accident, but also, and to an incalculably high degree, by the fact that Jesuits were responsible for the university's foundation and have been centrally involved in its daily life for these past two centuries. It is significant, I think, that in the five-year plan for the main campus approved by Georgetown's Board of Directors in 1982, the list of six major goals drawn up for this period of the university's history include the following: "to affirm and strengthen the Catholic and Jesuit character of Georgetown University; . . . to maintain our commitment to liberal education . . . ; to build a stronger sense of community—one dedicated to serve." The link between these goals, as I have tried to argue, is not a fortuitous one; it grows from that Jesuit fusion of humanism and mysticism that stands at the university's origin and that makes it still, to a great extent, what it is.

But the challenge of being what we are is no small one. Learning to find God in all things, becoming free enough to worship God for what he is and generous enough to serve him among his creatures: this Christian rereading of the education of free citizens is more challenging, more laborious, perhaps, than even its secular classical model, if only because we recognize more acutely that the one we seek in our contemplation of the world is wrapped in mystery. The Jesuit poet, Gerard Manley Hopkins, himself a student and later a professor of Greek literature, caught both the rapture and the labor of finding God in creatures in a stanza of his great theological poem, *The Wreck of the Deutschland:*

I kiss my hand
To the stars, lovely-asunder
Starlight, wafting him out of it; and
Glow, glory in thunder;
Kiss my hand to the dappled-with-damson west:

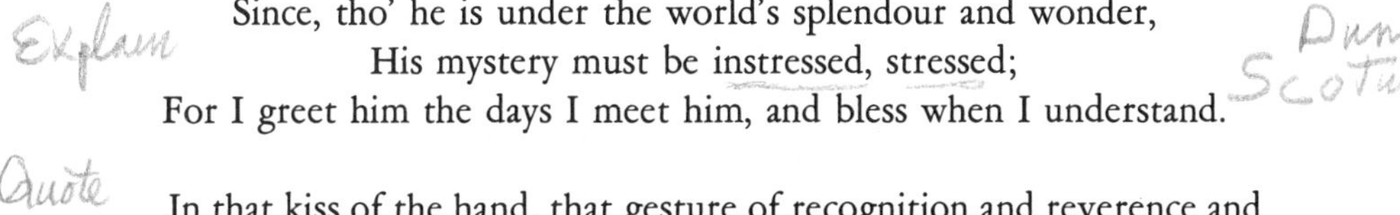

Since, tho' he is under the world's splendour and wonder,
His mystery must be instressed, stressed;
For I greet him the days I meet him, and bless when I understand.

In that kiss of the hand, that gesture of recognition and reverence and love toward the world's mysterious, often threatening beauty, pagan and Christian alike might find a sign that the poet's liberal education had left its mark. To the Christian, however—and especially to a Christian stamped by the "Jesuit character," trained in the mystical and practical prayer of the Ignatian *Exercises*—his kiss of the hand toward creatures, despite the stress, becomes more than simply a mark of insight; it becomes the sign of a personal encounter, an act of adoration and faith, a pledge of service. The distinctive goal of Georgetown University, surely, and of all its sister institutions marked with that Jesuit character, is nothing less, I think, than to offer to anyone ready to seek it the chance for such a meeting with the Lord.

Notes

1. Pedro de Ribadeneyra, S.J., *Tratado en el qual se da razón del instituto de la religión de la Compañia de Jesus* (Madrid: Colegio de la Compañia, 1605); translated into Latin by L. Carli, *De Ratione Instituti Societatis Jesu* (Rome: Civiltà cattolica, 1864). See J.-F. Gilmont, *Les écrits spirituels des premiers Jésuites* (Rome: Institutum Historicum S.I., 1961), 275.
2. de Ribadeneyra, *Tratado,* 510-19.
3. Ibid., 510.
4. Ibid.
5. Ibid.
6. Ibid.
7. Ibid., 518.
8. Ibid., 511.
9. Ibid., 511-15.
10. Ibid., 515f.

11. Ibid., 517.

12. Ibid.

13. Letter of May 21, 1547: *Monumenta Historica Societatis Jesu: Monumenta Ignatiana* I, 1 (Madrid: López del Horno, 1903), 519-26 (Ep. 174); trans. W.J. Young, S.J., *Letters of St. Ignatius Loyola* (Chicago: Loyola University Press, 1959), 132-37 (here, 136).

14. For the original Spanish text of the *Exercises,* as well as an early Latin translation and various early commentaries, see *Monumenta Historica Societatis Jesu: Exercitia Spiritualia* (Madrid: Successorum Rivadeneyrae, 1919). There are many modern English translations of the *Exercises.* Perhaps the most useful contemporary edition, containing (on facing pages) both the classic, literal translation by Elder Mullan, S.J., and a helpful modern paraphrase by David L. Fleming, S.J., is David. L. Fleming, S.J., ed., *The Spiritual Exercises: a Literal Translation and a Contemporary Reading* (St. Louis: Institute of Jesuit Sources, 1978).

15. *Spir. Ex.* 60; Mark 2:5.

16. For a contemporary theological discussion of the "mysticism" toward which the Ignatian *Exercises* are meant to lead, see Harvey D. Egan, S.J., *The Spiritual Exercises and the Ignatian Mystical Horizon* (St. Louis: Institute of Jesuit Sources, 1976).

17. *Spir. Ex.,* 230f.

18. Ibid., 234.

19. Ibid., 23.

20. For the text, see *Monumenta Historica Societatis Jesu: Constitutiones et Regulae Societatis Jesu* (4 vols.; Rome: Pontificiae Universitatis Gregorianae, 1934-48). The standard English translation now, with excellent introduction and notes, is George E. Ganss, S.J., *The Constitutions of the Society of Jesus* (St. Louis: Institute of Jesuit Sources, 1970).

21. *Const.* IV, 12: 446.

22. Ibid., 447.

23. Ibid., 450.

24. Ibid., 452.

25. The best modern survey of the history and early character of Jesuit education is George E. Ganss, S.J., *St. Ignatius' Idea of a Jesuit University* (Milwaukee: Marquette University Press, 1956); for the organization and teaching methods used in the early Jesuit colleges, see esp. pp. 44-111. See also John W. Donohue, S.J., *Jesuit Education. An Essay on the Foundations of Its Idea* (New York: Fordham University Press, 1963); and Mabel Lundberg, *Jesuitische Anthropologie und Erziehungslehre in der Frühzeit des Ordens (ca. 1540-ca. 1650)* (Uppsala: Almqvist & Wiksells, 1966).

26. *Constitutions* IV, 13:456.

27. Ibid.

28. *Constitutions* IV, 15:478.

29. Ibid.

30. Jerome Nadal, S.J., *Constitutiones Collegii Messanensis* (1548): *Monumenta Paedagogica Societatis Jesu* I, 2, 4 (= *Monumenta Historica Societatis Jesu* 92; Rome, 1965), 19f.; cf. *Constitutions* IV, 16:483.

31. *Const. Coll. Mess.* 5: *Mon. Paed. SJ* I, 20; *Constitutions* IV, 16:486.

32. *Const. Coll. Mess.* 6-7: *Mon. Paed. SJ* I, 20.

33. *Const. Coll. Mess.* 1, 3, 7: *Mon. Paed. SJ* I, 19f.; cf. *Constitutions* IV, 16:481.

34. *Constitutions* IV, 16:482.

35. *Const. Coll. Mess.* 13: *Mon. Paed. SJ* I, 21.

36. *Const. Coll. Mess.* 10: *Mon. Paed. SJ* I, 21.

37. *Const. Coll. Mess.* 14: *Mon. Paed. SJ* 21.

38. *Const. Coll. Mess.* 8, 9, 15: *Mon. Paed. SJ* I, 20f.; cf. *Constitutions* IV, 16:486.

39. *Constitutions* IV, 16:486.

40. *vir perfectae eloquentiae: Orator* 32 [113].

41. *Confessions* X, 22 [32]f.

42. *Institutio Oratoris, Praef.* 9f.

43. *Constitutions* III, 1: [288] 26.

44. *Const. Coll. Mess.* 11f.: *Mon. Paed. SJ* I, 21.

G. Ronald Murphy, S.J.

Georgetown's Shield: Utraque Unum

G. Ronald Murphy, S.J., is Associate Professor of German at Georgetown University and former Rector of the Jesuit Community.

I would like to talk tonight about Georgetown's spirit and its Jesuit character represented by the fascinating seal of the university. The shield fascinates me; the motto fascinates me; Georgetown fascinates me. I am not a historian but when I came here one of the first things I asked about was that shield. It was obvious to me, and I guess it is obvious to anyone looking at it, that the seal bears a noteworthy resemblance to the Great Seal of the United States. I believe the visual poetry of the Georgetown seal is intended to be analogous to the Great Seal of the United States. Before we can discuss the analogy, however, we need to dispense with the myths that distort the meaning of the imagery on our seal.

There is a great deal of mythology regarding the meaning of Georgetown's seal. The most prominent myth is that Georgetown University is the only university allowed to use the United States eagle on its coat of arms. It is said that we alone—aside from the military and naval academies—were given permission because we were founded at the same time as the new republic. Actually, it turns out that no permission was given, none was asked, and it is presumed that none is needed should anyone wish to duplicate Georgetown's use of the national emblem.

A second myth concerns our motto, *Utraque Unum* (Both are One). This is said to refer to the fact that Georgetown wished to have harmony between the Northern and the Southern states because our students were drawn from the Union and the Confederacy. To corroborate this myth, I was directed to Georgetown's colors—blue and gray. While it is true that our colors belong to attempts to heal the divisions of the Civil War era, both the shield and the motto have their origins far earlier. Historically and geographically, there is certainly some truth that Georgetown University unites both North and South; nevertheless, our motto is not rooted in the Civil War, but in the American Revolution.

The third myth is that the cross and the eagle stand for *Pro Deo et Patria*—for God and the Fatherland. There may be something to this interpretation in a broad cultural and even an historical sense, but I do not believe that is the intent of the the unknown person who drew this beautiful design for our coat of arms, since it does not do justice to much that is also expressed in the seal.

What can be determined about the origin of our seal/coat of arms? What do we actually know? One of the ways in which historians and archivists here have been a great help to me is to have determined the age of our seal by counting the stars displayed on it. There aren't thirteen, as one might expect, but sixteen.

It's entirely possible that the creator of the seal was perhaps attempting to do what our American flag does: keep up with the number of additional states added to the union by adding stars. There was a period when there were sixteen states—from 1796, when Tennessee was admitted to the Union as the sixteenth state—until 1803, when Ohio was admitted. We believe we can date our seal roughly between those dates of 1796 and 1803. Georgetown archivists have delved a little further, however, and found an entry in the school accounts for May 11, 1798, indicating a cash gift of fifteen shillings given to the university by the nurse for the younger students to pay "for the seal of the corporation."[1]

The nurse who gave this money was Joustine Douat. Interesting, because it is a French name and because she is known to have been a friend of Fr. DuBourg, who at that time served as the third president of the university. Our archivists also know—and I don't know how they found this out—that the French-speaking Joustine Douat and the French-speaking Jesuit president, Fr. DuBourg, loved to go to the theater together (accompanied, of course, by others). During one of these excursions it may well have been that the good Father mentioned the need for a certain subscription for some fifteen shillings. In any case, we know it was paid.

To add weight to this conclusion, it helps to know that both Fr. DuBourg and Joustine Douat came to Georgetown from Santo Domingo. This island in the Caribbean had been Spanish, but had recently come under French rule. Throughout the Spanish Empire at that time, east and west, a series of coins was minted bearing the inscription *Utraque Unum,* signifying the unity of Spain and its colonies, the two parts of the empire under one flag. This has been affirmed by the American Numismatic Society.

Where did this motto come from and did it originate on that coin which was minted in 1772? The words on the coin are an accommodated use of a phrase in the Vulgate version of Scripture—the Latin version of the day—taken from St. Paul's letter to the Ephesians, chapter 2, verse 14. In this passage St. Paul is determined to deliver the message that Christians, whether they be Gentiles or Jews, are one. He says:

> Therefore, remember at one time you were Gentiles in the flesh, you were called by the uncircumcision. But now remember, you were at that time

> separated from Christ, alienated from the commonwealth of Israel, but now you have hope in Christ Jesus. You who were once far off, have been brought near in the blood of Christ, for He is our peace, He has made us *utraque unum,* both one. He has abolished in His flesh the laws of commandments and ordinances that He might create a new man in the place of the two and thus make peace.

That, I believe, is the original context of our motto which was used in a second sense within the Spanish Empire, meaning that the people of the New and Old Worlds were one. It is used at the top of our university seal where the eagle carries in its beak a commenting allusion to the American eagle's message—*E pluribus unum* (From Many, One).

Is Fr. DuBourg the poet of our seal? No one really knows. Fr. DuBourg may well have paid for it by charming the money out of Joustine Douat, but we do not know if he actually designed the seal or even if he suggested the motto. One archivist waggishly suggested that he must have, for he was the only Jesuit with enough imagination in that time to have thought of it! Not knowing the exact identity of the poet does not prevent us from interpreting the seal, however. The unknown designer has provided us with several clues in the form of its visual allusion to the Great Seal of the United States and in its relation to Georgetown's spirit as expressed in the Prospectus of 1786, and in the seal's clear reflection of Jesuit educational character.

Let's consider first the American seal. Three of America's greatest sons of the Enlightenment—Benjamin Franklin, John Adams, and Thomas Jefferson—were commissioned on July 4, 1776 to design a great seal, a coat of arms for the infant United States of America. By the end of August they returned to Congress with a shield reminiscent of the rattlesnake cartoon of the revolution, in which the rattlesnake was shown cut into thirteen pieces underneath a motto, "Unite or die!" Instead of bits of rattlesnake, however, the thirteen original colonies were depicted as thirteen individual shields, each with an identifying initial. In the center of these shields were symbols representing the multiple nationalities of America—a fleur-de-lis for the French, a harp for the Irish, a double-headed eagle for the Germans, and so forth. Encompassing all the shields and symbols was a single great shield attesting to the unity of all—many had become one, and this was supported on either side by a man and a woman, a device common to coats of arms of the time.

I need hardly tell you that this first effort was rejected. It was ugly and overwrought. Yet the motto and the concept of national unity were not forgotten and, many transformations later, became clarified in the words *E pluribus unum* and in starry glory above the head of the American eagle as our new nation, represented by thirteen stars, would take its place as a new constellation. Critics who had wanted something fresher were pleased with the more visionary image of a free-soaring eagle. This clearly indicated our new nation was to hold itself aloft by its own power or, as they said in the language of those times, by its own "virtue." The United States of America was to soar like an eagle with its eye toward the sun, holding in its talons the sovereign right to declare peace or war.

The shield on the eagle's breast represents the thirteen original colonies: red stripes signifying courage; white stripes for innocence; the blue "chief" across the top representing justice and virtue. There are thirteen arrows in the eagle's talons and exactly thirteen leaves on the olive branch, clearly indicating that the ultimate responsibility for peace or war would lie in the hands of democratically elected persons.

Such noble ideals must have impressed John Carroll and the designer of Georgetown's shield, for our shield is an attempt to speak in the language of the new democracy. In the claws of Georgetown's eagle are not the arrows of war nor the olive branch of peace, but rather the cross of religion and the globe and calipers of science and knowledge, of learning and wisdom. Our shield says something as deeply as it can to the new nation in our nation's own language.

The tradition of speaking in the language of the country in which one dwells is a very old Jesuit tradition. Those of you who know the history of the Society of Jesus and its missionary efforts know that Jesuits are famous for having traveled to China, where they donned the robes of the mandarins and attempted to re-express Christianity in Chinese terms. Jesuits journeyed to Paraguay, speaking Guaraní, and attempted to create an Indian state free of interference and rule from the Spanish and Portuguese. It was not surprising that when the Jesuits came to these shores, therefore, they would attempt to speak "American"—a difficult language because our people did not settle here from republics and democracies but from wholly different, nontolerant systems—the absolutist monarchies of Europe.

John Carroll, founder of Georgetown and former Jesuit, was born not far from this spot in Upper Marlboro and attended Bohemia Manor on the Chesapeake Bay, one of Georgetown's ancestor schools. At age thirteen, he was sent across the ocean to St. Omer's, which was an English-speaking college in Flanders that formed clergy and educated English Catholic sons who could not be educated in the American colonies due to the suppression of the Catholic religion. (Carroll's parents, by the way, did not see him again for twenty-seven years.)

While in Europe, he completed his two-year Jesuit novitiate and was sent to Liège to begin the study of philosophy. In 1758 he returned to St. Omer's to teach the classics, a point I will return to. It was while he was teaching that the suppression of the Society of Jesus was decreed by the Parliament of Paris. St. Omer's was confiscated by force and transferred to the English secular clergy. The little student body was assembled and told the news and informed they must leave immediately for Bruges. Following their teaching masters out the doors of the college, they began the long journey without baggage. It took them three days of walking to arrive in Bruges. This was John Carroll's introduction, I believe, to the concept of *cujus regio, ejus religio,* i.e., whosoever's region it is, that's whose religion you are going to practice.

Carroll was twenty-seven at this time. He was ordained into the priesthood in 1769, by which time the Jesuits were being suppressed all over Europe—in Portugal, France, Spain, Naples, Parma—as well as in French Louisiana. The Society of Jesus had been deprived of its corporate existence throughout the Catholic world with the exception of two countries, Prussia and Russia (which did not recognize the brief of Clement XIV). During this time, Carroll made his first trip to Rome, accompanying a nobleman's young son. A few letters from this trip have survived. The Eternal City apparently chilled rather than inflamed his devotion. Rome then, as in more recent times, looked with such disfavor on the Jesuits that Carroll was compelled to conceal his background. He endeavored to see the Jesuit Fathers of his province who were personal friends, but they were away from Rome and thus he met no one in the Society.

All of this suppression and hostility and suspicion were due to European politics as much as religion. That is important to remember, for it affected John Carroll deeply. He resumed teaching when he returned to Bruges and on October 14, 1773, he and his colleagues were arrested when Austrian commissioners smashed down the doors and forced their way into the college. Upon his release, Carroll set out for England and began his long homeward journey to Maryland.

It is perhaps not surprising that he fell totally in love with the American solution to the problem of religion and politics. His American colleagues and contemporaries—Franklin, Adams, and Jefferson—were fighting for the disestablishment of all religions and for the free practice of any. During the American Revolution, Carroll was sent on a mission with Benjamin Franklin to the French Canadians, to assure them that it would be safe to join with the American revolution. The object was to assure the French Canadians that the Catholic religion would not be suppressed in an American alliance. Carroll was the perfect witness. At the conclusion of this mission, Carroll met with fellow Jesuits and proposed a new type of Roman Catholic university, one that had never existed on earth, one that would foster the new American principles based on the Enlightenment.

In the subsequent proposal for Georgetown University, we find the following prospect set out:

> The object of the proposed institution is to unite the means of communicating science with an effectual provision for guarding and preserving the morals of youth.[2]

"Morals" as understood in Carroll's time consisted of goodness, kindness, prudence, justice—the virtues which help make the students good men as well as learned men. There were thus two goals, not one. With this view, the *seminary* (as it was referred to then) would be superintended by those who, having had experience in similar institutions, knew that an undivided attention may be given *both* to the cultivation of virtue *and* to literary improvement—*utraque unum*—both, and—for they are both one. Carroll continued:

> And that a system of discipline may be introduced and preserved incompatible with inattention in the professor or with incorrigible habits of immorality by the students.[3]

Carroll incorporated two additional principles:

> The higher sciences shall be studied in this university so that the students may proceed to any of the universities in the neighboring states.[4]

There would be no need to go back to Europe for advanced education. What would be available at Georgetown would be calculated for every class of citizen. This was to be the first institution of real democracy. Georgetown was not to be a school for noblemen nor a school for the deathly poor. It was to be open to every class. Georgetown then and now embodies an eighteenth century ideal. Carroll's vision and his expression of that vision were not that America was a classless society, but rather that Georgetown would be accessible, in accordance with *American* principles, to all levels of society. That brings us to the question of religion. This is a Roman Catholic institution and yet Carroll said explicitly:

> Agreeable to the liberal principle of our Constitution, this seminary will be open to students of every religious profession.[5]

That statement has been part of our Georgetown tradition from the very beginning. We are open to every religion. These doors will never be smashed down by police, as they had been in Carroll's Europe. Carroll's statement says:

> They, who in this respect (i.e., religion) differ from the superintendent of the academy, they will be at liberty to frequent their places of worship.[6]

This was indeed revolutionary language. He was saying that anyone attending this Jesuit university would be granted liberty in accordance with the Constitution of this brand new revolutionary republic—liberty to attend and frequent the places of worship and instruction designated by the parents of the students. We are thus blessed with the wonderful image of Jesuits in those early years not only dragging Catholic boys out of bed and shoving them into Mass at five o'clock in the morning, but also of rousting Protestants and quick-marching them into the streets of Georgetown to *their own* churches: "Get in there! Your mother said so!" This was most definitely not *cujus regio, ejus religio!*

Carroll's final instructions were as follows:

> Though all are at liberty to attend and frequent their places of worship, . . . with respect for their moral conduct [again, in the eighteenth century, conduct where moral means humane and human virtuousness, their goodness and kindness toward one another and their moral virtue] all must be subject to the same general and uniform discipline.[7]

To put it somewhat more bluntly: "Don't tell me you can hit someone because your religion says you can; you *can't* hit him, period!" The entire school would follow the same rules of moral Christian behavior.

If we interpret what we see in our shield in the light of John Carroll's perspective, we begin to take on his mind, as it were. Is it "Jesuit"? I maintain that it most certainly is. In the *Constitutions of the Society of Jesus,* St. Ignatius wrote: "If we found a university, it is to be founded for one purpose only; we are to do it out of charity."[8] It is therefore to be an act of love. In his *Spiritual Exercises,* Ignatius informed the Jesuits in no uncertain terms what he thought love is. As I read his words, I like to consider John Carroll's great love for this fledgling republic to which he had returned after being arrested in Europe. Ignatius wrote:

> Love consists in mutual exchange on either side; that is to say, the lover giving and communicating to the beloved that which he has, that which he is able to give; and so, in turn, in the beloved making return to the lover.[9]

Ignatius further instructed: "If one should have knowledge, honors, riches, he should give it to him who has not."[10] This instruction was eagerly received by many of the gentlemen of the Enlightenment in this new country of ours. Franklin and Carroll became friends. George Washington, even though he was an Episcopalian and a Mason, delighted in having his grandnephews instructed by the Jesuit Fathers of Georgetown, and he visited them here.

So much, then, for the presence of the American eagle on our shield. What about the cross? In the light of what we know of the early days of our nation's founding, the cross should be interpreted as symbolizing religion in that eighteenth century sense—i.e., representing the practice of religion, the virtues of goodness and morality in personal and public life. At Georgetown it was not so much a question of which religion a student had as how he would practice it.

Can this strong American eagle hold the cross in one claw? Our shield challenges America not to establish a state religion, but to foster a climate where a citizen can be good, virtuous, and kind in an atmosphere of religious diversity and tolerance. Our university seal uses the eagle symbol of our nation as a protector of the ideal of faith.

St. Ignatius insisted that a spiritual person must realize that God dwells in all things and that he can be found in all things—in the stones, in the earth, in the plants and in the sea, in *oneself.* Ignatius further suggested that we consider how God works in all these things dynamically, causing them to be, move, and live, to interact and build. His final point is most significant and we rarely give sufficient reflection to it. He believed that the virtues themselves are as divine in origin as is the universe. This point was particularly close to the hearts of Enlightenment thinkers. Ignatius wrote:

> Contemplate how all good things and gifts descend from above us as, for example, my limited power comes from the supreme and infinite power on high. And in the same way, justice, goodness, pity, mercy, just as the rays descend from the sun and just as the water descends from the fountain.[11]

There can be no problem for a Jesuit university in recognizing in the nonbeliever the great virtues that descend from God himself. The cross in our seal therefore cannot be interpreted narrowly, but rather in an ecumenical sense, reflecting the tradition of the state of Maryland, which was the first of the colonies to originate the concept of real tolerance. Georgetown chose to describe itself as situated *ad ripas Potomaci in Marylandia* (on the banks of the Potomac in Maryland).

William Blake's great painting shows God creating the world, leaning down with calipers to measure, to set limits. Calipers are a real sign of the universe as envisioned by the men of the Enlightenment, men of reason. Incorporating the calipers and the globe into our seal is, I believe, an attempt to speak to these friends of reason and intellect—Franklin, Adams, Jefferson, and their followers—and thereby to state our belief that it is possible to study science, geology, navigation, surveying, and *simultaneously* to practice Christian virtue and to lead a virtuous and holy life. Students were to be trained in and for an informed and responsible nation and it was important that Georgetown make this statement early, clearly, publicly, and with conviction, on the very symbol of the college itself.

As the first principle and foundation of his spirituality, Ignatius wrote:

> Man was created to praise, to reverence, and to serve God, our Lord, and by this means to save his soul. All other things on the face of the earth were created for man's sake and in order to aid him in the prosecution of the end for which he was made.[12]

In the final meditation of the *Spiritual Exercises,* he wrote:

> Consider how God dwells in all of the creatures, in the elements giving them being, in the plants giving them growth, in the animals giving them sensation . . . [13]

How then could there be any religious difficulty with studying botany if God dwells in the plants; how any difficulty with geology if he dwells in the rocks; how could there be any difficulty in anthropology or in literature if he dwells in humankind? In Jesuit spirituality there is no problem with holding the cross and the calipers simultaneously. This is not always the case in other traditions.

Catholic universities founded in the nineteenth century were founded by later immigrants who had not participated in the Revolution or in the founding of the new republic. They came a few decades later with particular ethnic and religious values to protect from inculturation, into an environment that had become more hostile. This later development emphasizes all the more Georgetown's unique origin. Certain fundamentalist universities and colleges today maintain the separation of the cross and the calipers. I have seen one representative of another faith appear on television and assert that he would not allow what the microscope shows to be taught if what it shows is not "biblical." In our tradition there is nothing that a telescope or a microscope can show that could be nonbiblical if God is the creator of all things.

If you walk up Georgetown's western hill and turn to the left, you will find a beautiful old path. At the crest of the hill, in the middle of this Roman Catholic university, you will find an observatory with whose very calipers the longitude of Washington, D. C. was first determined and where official time was "set" for the capital and for the United States. The observatory is situated in a garden where botanical experiments were once conducted by a famous priest/scientist, Fr. Frank Heyden, S.J.

As we all know, universities that embrace only the globe and the calipers can—and do—ignore or reject the cross. When I was studying at Harvard, I remember walking through one of the old gates and looking up and seeing something that startled me. I had always assumed that Harvard's motto was simply *Veritas* (Truth), and that this limited Harvard's teaching responsibility to microscope, telescope, calipers, and globe. But my excursion through the old gate revealed Harvard's original coat of arms under the ivy: *Pro Christo et Ecclesia*—For Christ and the Church!

What had happened to change their vision and their direction? Couldn't they hold both values together? Georgetown's pride is that we opt both for *veritas* and *pro Christo et Ecclesia.* Our coat of arms proclaims an ideal of balance and integration. How do we hold both these values together? That is shown at the very top of the shield. You will recall that the Great Seal of the United States depicts the American dream of the unity of the colonies represented by the circle of stars above the eagle's head. In a parallel format, Georgetown's seal depicts not a constellation, but a lyre. A lyre, as you know, has many strings, each sounding a different note. The strings of the lyre are symbols for science and religion and literature and government; each, when plucked, sounds a different note. But together they make a harmony; they are held together in harmony.

Which brings us to the question which is to me perhaps the most intriguing of all surrounding the origin of our shield: Why was a lyre selected above all else to represent the harmony among all things? I have an idea that I offer for your consideration. John Carroll taught the classics, as you know. One of the things about his life that intrigues me is that he studied and taught in a place called St. Omer's. I have often wondered if the mystery hidden in the shield of Georgetown might not lie somehow or other in that lyre.

If you look carefully at our seal, the globe is not particularly glorified. There are no rays of light shining around it. Even the cross is just plainly there as a cross. But in the Greek lyre of the humane—the arts understood as the humane—the music of human aspiration is glorified. It is a clue to the great harmony and unity that Georgetown aspires to have and to offer: the striving of the humane scientist to improve life for others, not the power plays of political fanatics; it is the ongoing discernment of the person of faith, not the flippant greed of the overly competitive. The truly humane is what is created by God. It is the source of virtue and the source of scientific inquiry. It is the source of goodness and wisdom. Our beautiful lyre speaks to all that is best and most harmonious in human dreaming and discourse and discovery.

In conclusion, I hope you won't mind if I read from Homer, one of my favorite authors, from the *Iliad,* in which this ideal of human harmony is portrayed in eloquent simplicity. I have treated some of the faculty to this before. Be patient with me; I love this epic poem very much. Homer is believed to have written about 750 years before the birth of Christ. The *Iliad* contains a great and frighteningly moving description of warfare and its aftermath, so well done that it absorbs the reader totally. At the end one waits for the glorious fall of Troy, perhaps for the great wooden horse to be wheeled in and for might to triumph. But there is no Trojan horse at the end of the *Iliad.* One waits for the collapse of the city, but there is no collapse. This powerful tale, speaking across the centuries, ends in a way simultaneously to shame us and to enlighten us, to make us all very proud of our capacity to love and forgive.

The two great heroes of the story have come into conflict, Achilles for the Greeks and Hector for the Trojans. Hector is defeated and Achilles, blind with fury over what Hector had done to his friends, has Hector tied to the back of his chariot and drags the body three times around the wall of the entire city of Troy. Hector's body bumps and smashes against the rocks. It is covered with dirt, blood-smeared, abused almost beyond recognition. Achilles then retires from the walls of Troy but, to make his contempt absolute, he commands that Hector's body be exposed where it is certain to be eaten and disappear into the stomachs of hyenas, dogs, and vultures, depriving this warrior forever of even the hope of a shadowy afterlife. It is the ultimate insult, the ultimate horror, the ultimate deprivation.

Hector's father, Priam, the elderly king of Troy, has seen all of this from the walls of the city. Troy has suffered through ten years of warfare and now has been defeated and debased. By any human measurement, all has been lost. But Priam now does an amazing thing. He leaves the city in secret and goes humbly to his enemy of enemies, to Achilles, for the sake of his son, Hector. This is how Homer concludes the story of the famous Trojan war:

> Big though the king was, Priam, he crept into the tent of Achilles unobserved and, before anyone could do anything, he ran up to Achilles, he grasped his knees, he kissed his hands—the terrible man-killing hands that had slaughtered so many of his sons.
>
> Achilles was astounded when he saw the king, Priam, and so were all of his men; they looked at each other in amazement. But Priam was already praying to Achilles: "Most worshipful Achilles," he said, "think of your own father who is the same age as I, and who has nothing but miserable old age ahead of him. No doubt his neighbors are oppressing him and there's nobody to save him. But at least he has one consolation—while he knows

> that you are still alive, he can look forward day by day to seeing his beloved son come back from Troy—whereas my fortunes are completely broken. I had the best of sons in this whole land and not one, not one, is left. All have fallen in action, and Hector—the only one I could still count on—the bulwark of Troy, has now been killed by you, fighting for his native land. It is to get him back from you that I have come here to the Achaean ships. Achilles, fear the gods, be merciful to me. Remember your own father, even though I am more entitled to compassion since I have brought myself to do a thing no one on earth has ever done. I have raised my lips to the hands of the man who killed my son."
>
> Priam had set Achilles thinking of his own father and brought him to the verge of tears. Taking the old man's hand, he gently put him from him and, overcome by their memories, they both broke down. Priam, crouching at Achilles' feet, wept bitterly for his son Hector and Achilles wept for his father and for his friend Patroclus, and the house was filled with the sound of their lamentation. But when they had had enough of their tears and recovered, Achilles leapt from his chair and, in compassion for the old man's gray hairs and his beard, took him by the arm and he raised him and returned his son.[14]

This is supposedly *pagan* literature, extolling compassion, humane relationships between human beings. The poet praises harmony even between those thought to be mortal enemies.

This is close indeed to what St. Paul was trying to do in his letter to the Ephesians when he begged Christians who were Greek and Christians who were Jews to cease fighting among themselves, pleading *utraque unum,* you are both one.

Is it not possible in humane Jesuit Georgetown education to hold both Paul and Homer—both cross and calipers—together, and say to Jefferson, to Washington, to Franklin, "Utraque Unum—we can hold faith and reason in the harmony of the human"?

One final observation. All John Carroll's study and teaching, until the Jesuits were forced to disband, had been done at a college which the English Jesuits named—and had not hesitated to name—St. Omer's. As you know, the English often drop their 'h's' in pronunciation. St. Omer is really St. Homer. In a sense, the great-great-grandfather of Georgetown University is a small college where John Carroll taught the humanities and was taught by them, whose very name reveals that virtue and sanctity should be acknowledged wherever and in whatever human author they are found, a small college in the fields of exile called *St. Omer's*.

Notes

1. Archives, Georgetown University, Washington, D.C.
2. John M. Daley, S.J., *Georgetown University: Origin and Early Years* (Washington, D.C.: Georgetown University Press, 1959), 34.
3. Ibid., 35.
4. Ibid.
5. Ibid.
6. Ibid.
7. Ibid.
8. *The Constitutions of the Society of Jesus,* translated with introduction and a commentary by George E. Ganss, S.J. (St. Louis: The Institute of Jesuit Sources, 1970), 210.
9. *Spiritual Exercises of St. Ignatius,* trans. Louis J. Puhl, S.J. (Chicago: Loyola University Press, 1951), 101.
10. Ibid.
11. Ibid., 103.
12. Ibid., 12.
13. Ibid., 102.
14. Homer, *The Iliad,* trans. E.V. Riess (Baltimore: Penguin Books, 1966), 450-51.

WALTER J. BURGHARDT, S.J.

Fat Cats or Suffering Servants? Georgetown University and the Faith That Does Justice

WALTER J. BURGHARDT, S.J., is Theologian in Residence at Georgetown University and editor of the journal *Theological Studies.*

To do at least minimal justice to the issue I have raised ("Fat Cats or Suffering Servants?"), I must address myself to three areas, three subjects for reflection: (1) a culture and a counterculture, (2) the Christian basis for the counterculture, and (3) the future of the counterculture. Phrasing my approach another way, I shall cast a swift look (1) directly at today, (2) back at yesterday, and (3) forward to tomorrow. I shall, therefore, play successively the observer, the theologian, and the prophet.

I

First, the observer. A quarter century ago, a distinguished sociologist, Philip Rieff, saw a fresh character ideal coming to dominate Western civilization. Over against the ancient pagan commitment to the polis, to public life, over against the Judeo-Christian commitment to a transcendent God, over against the Enlightenment commitment to the irresistible progress of reason, the new ideal type was "anti-heroic, shrewd, carefully counting his satisfactions and dissatisfactions, studying unprofitable commitments as the sins most to be avoided."[1] The "highest science"? Self-concern.[2] Devotion and self-sacrifice? "Constraining ideals" that must be rejected.[3] "Spiritual guidance" in the best Freudian sense is "to emancipate man's 'I' from the communal 'we'."[4] Learn Freud's realism: conflict is embedded in human living, expectations are inevitably frustrated, life can have no all-embracing meaning, death is final.

Twenty-seven years have passed, and the situation Rieff described has apparently been aggravated. As respected a sociologist as Robert Bellah finds in our fair land a frightening phenomenon: a resurgence of late-nineteenth-century rugged individualism. American society is indeed moving away from religious man/woman, away from political man/woman, as character ideals. Those ideals were oriented to the public world, the community, the common good, the other. But when the central institution in our society is no longer religion or the political order but the economy, the ideal is now economic man/woman, man and woman in pursuit of private self-interest. Listen to Bellah:

> What is significant here is not the Moral Majority...but something that comes closer to being amoral and is in fact a majority. This new middle class believes in the gospel of success 1980 style. It is an ethic of how to get ahead

> in the corporate bureaucratic world while maximizing one's private goodies. In the world of the zero-sum society it is important to get to the well first before it dries up, to look out for number one, to take responsibility for your own life and keep it, while continuing to play the corporate game. . . . [5]

This new ideal, we are told, finds its strength in the younger generations. The dominant theme researchers find in young economic man/woman is freedom, autonomy, personal fulfillment; your sole responsibility is to yourself; in the end you're alone. The race is to the swift, the shrewd, the savage; and the devil take the hindmost.

Now what sociologists claim to have uncovered is dramatically illustrated by one illustrious educational institution. In 1986 Harvard University celebrated its 350th anniversary. The cover story in *Time* reported a sobering admission from Harvard's president. Incoming students are requested to state their three top goals (including, I presume, for life *after* Cambridge). What were the three top goals declared by the class of 1990? (1) Money, (2) power, (3) reputation.[6]

Is Harvard unique? Not if we can credit a recent survey sponsored by the American Council on Education and UCLA.[7] Who were surveyed? Nearly 290,000 incoming students in more than five hundred colleges and universities. The overall conclusion? "America's brightest young people" are "interested more than ever primarily in making money."

> Being "well off financially" now tops the list of "essential or very important" reasons for going to college. To "develop a meaningful philosophy of life," which used to rank high (nearly 83 percent in 1966), is now the lowest it has been in the 20-year history of the annual survey (39.4 percent). . . . [8]

Back in 1971, only 49.9 percent listed money as important; in the latest survey, financial success came up first for 75.6 percent. In harmony with this dramatic shift, "Business has become the No.1 college major, while interest in English and the humanities has fallen sharply, with teaching registering the greatest decline of all."[9]

Quite in line with such research is a documentary in the February 1988 issue of *Esquire,* authored by Joseph Nocera (currently at work on a book about the rise of money culture). Its title? "The Ga-Ga Years." Its subtitle? "Money love, market lust, and the seducing of America."[10] Nocera is "standing in a posh storefront in Manhattan, at the corner of Fifty-first Street and Park Avenue . . . the New York beachhead of Fidelity Investments . . . staring up at an electronic board . . . spewing out the current value of Fidelity's Select funds. . . . At the bottom of the board flashes the most dazzling prop of all: the Dow itself." Nocera comments: "If money is the new sex—and isn't that what everyone is saying these days?—then this place is the whorehouse."[11]

If money is the new sex. . . .

But if such is the dominant American culture, is there a counterculture that refuses to succumb? I believe there is. The temptation of the Geritol generation is to see the New Breed of the 1980s as irresponsible and undisciplined, uncommitted and uncaring, heedless of God and skeptical of church, devoid of doctrine and devotion. The indictment seems far too sweeping. The change in religious consciousness that sociologist Andrew Greeley has discovered among Catholic teen-agers, a transformation he believes is the result of reforms instituted by the Second Vatican Council, will startle the pessimist and delight the optimist. Hear his own summary statement:

> The New Breed of the 1980's is more likely to think of God as a mother and a lover, and of heaven as a life of action and pleasure. Its story of its love affair with God, and thus the meaning of its life, represents a dramatic change in Catholic religious sensibility, a change apparently caused by Vatican Council II and transmitted by devout mothers, sympathetic parish priests and passionately loving spouses. Because of this new vision of God and of life, the New Breed is more likely to be open to church careers, more socially committed, more insistent on high quality church performance by the church, more formal in their prayer, more concerned about racial justice, and more personally devout (but not more committed to the church's sexual teaching or to infallibility . . .). Their personal devotion may sag during the alienation interlude in the middle-20's, but the rest of their new religious sensibility is likely to remain unaltered.[12]

More socially committed. . . . My decade at Georgetown confirms this. I am not about to affirm that the Hilltop I survey is immune to the ills, to the materialism, I sketched above. Gather ten thousand adolescents and young adults on one campus from every state in the Union and beyond, and you are bound to find the prevailing culture heavily represented. And still, on the level of social action, hundreds upon hundreds of Hoyas leave me breathless in admiration. Take the Community Action Coalition. They reach out to the elderly: visits, happy hours, field trips, exercise classes, reading for the blind. They reach out to the underprivileged: the handicapped, the mentally ill. They reach out to the homeless: staff shelters, work in day centers, do advocacy work for tenants, lobby for street people. They reach out to battered women, to the raped and downtrodden. They reach out to the young: tutor the retarded and the delinquent, serve as role models and friends. They reach out to the Hispanic community: help them adapt, tutor them and translate, prepare them for citizenship.

Take CIPRA, the Center for Immigration Policy and Refugee Assistance. Some 200 Hoyas tutor recently arrived immigrant children in the District of Columbia school system. More than 500 GU students have worked as administrative interns with refugee agencies. Graduate students in business administration train Vietnamese who were successful in Vietnam to do business effectively in the United States. More than 250 fourth-year medical students have worked in refugee camps in Thailand. Forty-or-so GU students are tutoring thirty juvenile offenders who otherwise would be sentenced to detention in juvenile correction facilities. And so on and so forth.

Take the service program of Alpha Phi Omega Mu Alpha. Here you have some 150 brother-hours each week, hands outstretched to mentally handicapped Boy Scouts, to the Sunday meal at Zacchaeus Soup Kitchen, to night shifts at Mt. Carmel Women's Shelter, to odd jobs for the Little Sisters of the Poor.

A culture, yes: a rising tide of materialism. But a counterculture as well: a surging wave of service.

II

I move now from observer to theologian. Does a church committed to eternal salvation have anything to do with everyday justice? Does the Catholic Church, precisely as church, have a mission that includes justice and human rights? Does the church have a role to play in the social, political, and economic orders?[13]

Uncounted Christians, countless Catholics, shout a resounding no. As they see it, the church, as church, has *no* commission to right human injustice. The church is a spiritual institution, and its mission is sheerly spiritual; it is a channel that links woman and man with God. The church's charge is to help us know, love, and serve God in this life and enjoy God for ever in the next. Oh yes, poverty and politics, injustice and inhumanity may stand as barriers to God's grace. If they are, then the church must struggle against them. But not as a direct facet of its mission—only as obstacles at the outer edge of its vocation. The church's commission is to gather a band of true believers who will prepare themselves by faith and hope for the redemptive action by which God will establish the kingdom at the end of history.

Some who espouse this position appeal to the New Testament, to the Son of God in flesh. A letter from Texas once took social activist George G. Higgins to task for his views on the church and social justice. Christ "did not relieve suffering," the correspondent declared; he simply forgave sins. In consequence, the church should not be concerned about violations of social justice. Like Christ, it should concentrate on showing us that "it is the hardness of men's hearts that causes our suffering" and that "as long as the angel of darkness roams the world in search of souls and men fail to reject sin, human misery will continue to exist."[14] Along similar lines, there are Christians who insist that Christ taught a personal rather than a social morality.

Against such a privatized, me-and-Jesus religion the best of Catholic tradition cries out clearly, at times passionately. Papal pronouncements from Leo XIII's *Rerum novarum* (on the rights and obligations of workers, employers, and the state) to John Paul II's address at Puebla, his first encyclical (*Redemptor hominis*), later statements in North America and the Third World, and especially his recent encyclical on social concerns (*Sollicitudo rei socialis*), give the lie to such a thesis.

Oh indeed, the Christian has to avoid two extremes. On the one hand, salvation is not sheer socialization, personality development, liberation from oppressive structures, an end to poverty; it is a divinization, transformation into Christ. As the Fathers of the Church never tired of iterating, the Son of God became human to make humans divine—in their strong term, to make us "gods." The church's primary task is to see to it that the human person is refashioned in the image of Christ; short of this there is no salvation. God fulfills us by uniting us with God. The essential liberation is freedom from the slavery that is sin. As Pius XII said in a 1956 allocution, "The goal which Christ assigns to [the church] is strictly religious. . . . The church must lead men and women to God, in order that they may give themselves over to God unreservedly. . . ."[15]

On the other hand, any program of evangelization is inadequate if the church does not spend itself to free the human person from every inhuman shackle. I grant, the church has good news to preach even to those whose situation is humanly hopeless; for *the* good news is Jesus—Jesus alive, yearning to make those who are heavy-burdened one with him. Sanctity is possible in poverty-ridden Appalachia, in the icy exile of Siberia, in the apartheid of South Africa, in the excrement of Calcutta. But this does not exempt the People of God from the ceaseless struggle to transform the city of man and woman into the kingdom of God—a kingdom of peace, of justice, of love.

This is the vision that emerged from the Second Vatican Council—resoundingly in its *Decree on the Apostolate of the Laity:*

> Christ's redemptive work, while of its nature directed to the salvation of men and women, involves also the renewal of the whole temporal order. The Church has for mission, therefore, not only to bring to men and women the message of Christ and his grace, but also to saturate and perfect the temporal sphere with the spirit of the gospel. . . . The two spheres [spiritual and temporal], distinct though they are, are so linked in the single plan of God that he himself purposes in Christ to take up the whole world again into a new creation, initially here on earth, completely on the last day.[16]

This is the vision of the 1971 Synod of Bishops in its message "On Justice in the World": The vindication of justice and participation in the process of transforming the world is "a constitutive element of the preaching of the gospel."[17] This is the vision that emerged from the 1974 Synod of Bishops in a significant statement on "Human Rights and Reconciliation." Said the bishops in common:

> Human dignity is rooted in the image and reflection of God in each of us. It is this which makes all persons essentially equal. The integral development of persons makes more clear the divine image in them. In our time the Church has grown more deeply aware of this truth; hence she believes firmly that the promotion of human rights is required by the gospel and is central to her ministry.[18]

And in 1976, the International Theological Commission (an advisory body serving the pope), in a very carefully articulated examination of "Human

Development and Christian Salvation," argued that God's grace should sharpen the conscience of Christians, should help us build a more just world. Not simply by spiritual reformation; not simply by assisting individuals;

> for there is a kind of "injustice that assumes institutional shape," and as long as this obtains, the situation itself calls for a greater degree of justice and demands reforming. Our contemporaries are no longer convinced that social structures have been predetermined by nature and therefore are "willed by God," or that they have their origin in anonymous evolutionary laws. Consequently, the Christian must ceaselessly point out that the institutions of society originate also in the conscience of society, and that men and women have a moral responsibility for these institutions.
>
> We may argue how legitimate it is to speak of "institutional sin" or of "sinful structures," since the Bible speaks of sin in the first instance in terms of an explicit, personal decision that stems from human freedom. But it is unquestionable that by the power of sin injury and injustice can penetrate social and political institutions. That is why . . . even situations and structures that are unjust have to be reformed.
>
> Here we have a new consciousness, for in the past these responsibilities could not be perceived as distinctly as they are now. . . . [19]

More pointedly still, on December 30, 1987, John Paul II's encyclical on social concerns stated that "the Church's social doctrine adopts a critical attitude toward both liberal capitalism and Marxist collectivism," argued that "the conflicts . . . between East and West [are] an important cause of the retardation or stagnation of the South," claimed that "each of the two blocs harbors in its own way a tendency toward imperialism . . . or toward forms of neo-colonialism. . . ."[20]

Indeed, the Catholic vision of God's kingdom—a kingdom of peace and justice and love—is not limited to the last day, to the final coming of Christ. Still, as the International Theological Commission recognized, we Christians "have a new consciousness." Not that the Old Testament and the New are silent on social issues. Those who read in Scripture a sheerly personal morality have not sung the Psalms or been burned by the prophets, have not perceived the implications of Jesus' message.[21]

Take the prophets. Through Isaiah and Hosea, through Amos and Micah and Jeremiah, Yahweh ceaselessly tells Israel that he rejects just those things they think will make him happy. He is weary of burnt offerings, does not delight in the blood of bulls or lambs. Incense is an abomination to him. Their appointed feasts his soul hates. Their prayers and the melody of their harps he will not listen to. He does not want rivers of oil, thousands of rams, even their first-born. Then what is left? What can Yahweh possibly want? Two things: their steadfast love and that they execute justice (cf. Is 1:11-18; 42:1-4; Hos 2:18-20; 6:6; Am 5:18-25; Mi 6:6-8; Jer 7:5-7).

Now the justice God asked of Israel was not an ethical construct. It did not merely mean: Give to each what is due to each, what each person has a strict right to demand, because he or she is a human being, has rights that can be proven by philosophy or have been written into law. What, then, was the justice God wanted to "roll down like waters" (Am 5:24)? Justice was a whole web of relationships that stemmed from Israel's covenant with God. The Israelites were to father the fatherless and feed the sojourner, not because the orphan and the outsider deserved it, but because this was the way *God* had acted with *them.* A text in Deuteronomy is telling: "Love the sojourner, therefore; for you were sojourners in the land of Egypt" (Dt 10:19). In freeing the oppressed, they were mirroring the loving God who had delivered *them* from oppression, had freed them from Pharaoh. In loving the loveless, the unloved, the unlovable, they were imaging the God who wooed Israel back despite her infidelities, betrothed her to himself for ever (cf. Hos 2:14-23).

Justice, for the Jew, was not a question simply of human deserving, of human law. The Jews were to give to others what they had been given by God, were to act toward one another as God had acted toward them—and precisely because God had acted this way. Their justice was to image not the justice of man but the justice of God. For Israel, the practice of justice was an expression of steadfast love—God's love and their own love. Not to execute justice was not to worship God.

This is the tradition that sparked the ministry of Jesus: "I will put my Spirit upon him, and he shall proclaim justice to the Gentiles. . . . He will not break a bruised reed or quench a smoldering wick, till he brings justice to victory" (Mt 12:18-20). In harmony with Hosea, he wants not sacrifice but compassion, mercy (cf. Mt 12:7; 23:23). And the just man or the just woman is not primarily someone who gives to another what that other *deserves.* The just man, the just woman has covenanted with God; this covenant demands that we treat other human persons as *God* wants them treated in his covenant plan, treat friend and enemy as he treats them. And how does he treat them? He "makes his sun rise on the evil and on the good, sends rain on the just and on the unjust" (Mt 5:45).

The early Christians seem to have grasped that. If *anyone* is hungry or athirst, naked or a stranger, sick or in prison, it is always Christ who clamors for bread or water, Christ who cries to be clothed or welcomed, Christ whom you visit on a bed of pain or behind bars (cf. Mt 25:31-46).[22] And the First Letter of John is terribly uncompromising: "If anyone has the world's goods and sees his brother in need, yet closes his heart against him, how does God's love abide in him?" (1 Jn 3:17).

For all this remarkable tradition, it still remains true that the church has grown in its awareness of what Jeremiah's "execute justice" (Jer 7:5) and the gospel of love demand. It is in line with this growth that John Paul II confirmed contemporary magisterial teaching when in 1979 he told the Third General Assembly of the Latin American Bishops in Puebla: "The church has learned [in the pages of the gospel] that its evangelizing mission has as indispensable part (*como parte indispensable*) action for justice and those efforts which the development of the human person demands. . . . "[23]

As recent examples of the church's growth in understanding its proper involvement in sociopolitical and socioeconomic issues, I could cite and discuss the pastoral letters of the U.S. bishops on peace[24] and on the economy[25]—both of which have provoked strong reactions of approval and disapproval.[26] But I prefer, for our purposes, a still more dramatic example: the role played by the bishops of the Philippines in the presidential election of February 1986. Toward the end of that month, despot Ferdinand Marcos left a land he had despoiled for decades, and a Philippines in bondage recaptured its freedom. It recaptured its freedom in large measure because the Catholic Bishops' Conference of the Philippines had declared that "the polls were unparalleled in the fraudulence of their conduct": in the systematic disenfranchisement of voters, widespread and massive vote-buying, deliberate tampering with the election returns, intimidation, harassment, terrorism, and murder. It recaptured its freedom because the same bishops had proclaimed: "A government that assumes or retains power through fraudulent means has no moral basis. We do not advocate a bloody, violent means of righting this wrong. The way indicated to us now is active resistance by peaceful means—in the manner of Christ."[27] It recaptured its freedom because a cardinal called uncounted thousands to the streets to arrest tanks of war with rosaries and marigolds, with orchids and their unarmed bodies.

That cardinal, Jaime L. Sin, fourteenth of sixteen children of a Filipina mother and a Chinese father, told the story with incomparable persuasiveness in a 1986 commencement address at Georgetown University. The ceaseless theme of his address: The Catholic Church in the Philippines has been accused of interfering in politics. But the church was simply defending the human rights of the people. It was the state that was interfering with human rights: e.g., people driven off their land by the military; a priest (one of my theology students in the 1950s at the Jesuit seminary in Maryland) shot through the heart at six inches for championing their cause.

Sin was accused of interfering in politics because he wrote a pastoral letter to his people: Not "Vote for Cory" or "Vote for Marcos," but "Vote honestly . . . according to your conscience!" Because he wrote to his people about bribery: "Do not sell your vote. But if anyone offers you money, take it . . . and vote according to your conscience, according to your heart. Take the five pesos (25 cents). Buy rice for your children, buy fish, buy milk for the baby." How justify taking the pesos? "The money is yours anyway; it was stolen from the people."

> Look at these poor people! Twelve in one little room. At night they cannot sleep lying flat, because there is not enough room. They must sleep on their side, or else the twelve will not fit in that one little room. They do not eat properly, even once a day. Some live on food that they salvage from the garbage heaps.

In another pastoral letter, Sin pleaded with those in charge of the counting: "Please, do not cheat! Let the votes of the people be counted!" The appeal worked: thirty of the computer operators walked out, "because what they were putting into the computers was not coming out in the official tally."

When Sin asked the people to go out into the streets, to Camp Crame, to get between the 301 anti-Marcos soldiers and the advancing tanks, "They came out! At once! They filled the streets! They met the tanks! They put flowers into the muzzles of the rifles. The nuns knelt in front of the tanks and prayed the rosary. Schoolchildren linked arms and stood in front of the trucks—and the trucks were filled with armed soldiers. It was wonderful!" Was this interference in politics?

> I do not think that it was. If we did not do that, the tanks would have attacked Camp Crame, the planes would have bombed the troops that were besieged, the mortars would have shelled Ramos and Enrile from Camp Aguinaldo—and Manila would be now in a state of civil war. We would have had carnage from Aparri to Jolo. We did what the gospel told us to do. We stopped hatred with love. We stopped violence with prayer, with laughter, with confidence in the natural goodness of every man. I *knew* that the Filipino soldier would never fire on defenseless women and children. I was *sure* of that! That is why I sent our people out into the streets. . . .
>
> I think that the script for the Philippine elections in February, and the script for our revolution, was written by God.

I agree. I was privileged to write the citation for Cardinal Sin's honorary degree at Georgetown, privileged to close the citation with these words:

> In honoring this contemporary "prince of peace," Georgetown recognizes a powerful symbol of Christian reconciliation: ever a mediator with Marcos but never an accomplice, ever the passionate protester but never the reckless rebel, an inspiration to the fearful and the tearful. For reminding us masterfully that authority is service, that politics can be priestly, and that marigolds might be mightier than the sword, the President and Directors of Georgetown University with great pride and admiration proclaim His Eminence Jaime L. Cardinal Sin Doctor of Humane Letters, honoris causa.

III

So far so good. I have played the observer, have cast a swift look directly at today, have addressed myself to our culture and our counterculture. And I have played the theologian, have looked back at yesterday, have addressed myself to the Christian basis for our counterculture. Finally, let me play the prophet, look forward into your future, ask whether the counterculture I have described and tried to justify holds a future for *you.*

Indeed it should. For the ideal of human living espoused by economic man/woman I call deadly. I am aware of the seductive arguments. To serve others responsibly, you had better have your own act together, get your head screwed on right. To help the underdeveloped, you must develop your own mature individuality. To give intelligently, you should have something worth giving. Before you give, you must be. Integration before self-donation.

I am moved but not convinced. A world where a billion go to bed hungry and human rights are blasted, a world where more innocents are aborted each year than perished in two world wars, a world where war is always raging somewhere and panic walks the streets, a world where terrorism brings nations to a helpless halt and atomic destruction hangs overhead, a world where "crack" is king and the new great plague is AIDS, a world where uncounted thousands sleep the winter away on city grates or in homeless shelters, a world where politicians and preachers and entrepreneurs play games with ethics—this world cannot wait for collegians and yuppies to get their whole act together. I dare not tell anyone precisely what to do: dole out dinner at a soup kitchen, picket the Pentagon, scatter the slum landlords, clean out the inside traders, light the minds of retarded or refugee children. I *am* saying that if Georgetown's normal product is a woman or man simply of enlightened self-interest, GU's bicentennial should be its swan song.

The problem is, Christian social action may well be more difficult after commencement than before. Why? To begin with, your responsibilities will increasingly grow, widen, deepen; relationships will become more complex—husband or wife, children, work or professional school, home and finances, even paying off your Georgetown mortgage. Despite all this, GU grads do pack off to the poor in Peru, join the Jesuit Volunteers here, in Belize, in Nepal, in Micronesia. In New York City, lawyers, doctors, nurses, men and women of business help Franciscan Bruce Ritter at Covenant House, where some 12,000 runaway youngsters pass through each year—pimped, angel-dusted, scarred in flesh and spirit.

Even more of a problem is the possibility that you may be swallowed up by the dominant culture. Robert Bellah has suggested that one significant solution to our resurgent rugged individualism lies in the People of God, what St. Paul called the Body of Christ. As Bellah put it,

> . . . only the church as a type of Christian social organization can effectively combat the radical individualism and the managerial manipulativeness of modern society. . . . The church as the body of Christ can remind us that we will survive only insofar as we care for one another. As Christians and as

> citizens, we might just possibly recover an idea of the common good, of that which is good in itself and not just the good of private desire.[28]

As Christians. Not by private piety but precisely as a people, as a living body where if I hurt, you weep; if I joy, you laugh; if I die, you are diminished. The tragedy is, sympathetic scholars tell us, our Catholic body in America has been more conditioned by the culture than an influence upon it.

The crucial question is: How ready are you to resist the culture? In all the professions there are already individuals who do—and many of them were shaped by Georgetown. But Don Quixotes will not change the controlling culture. The culture will change only if educated men and women in massive numbers carry their Christianity into marketplace and counting house, into law court and genetics lab, conscious of their solidarity with every man, woman, and child "redeemed not with silver or gold but with the precious blood of Christ" (1 Pt 1:18-19). Not to fashion a Christian economics—that would be a two-headed monster—but to make economic man/woman serve the human person. Paradoxically, only thus will your profession be your servant, not you its slave.

Actually, my hopes are high. And this on the basis of almost a decade as theologian-in-residence at Georgetown. The experience has not indeed been all of a piece. On the one hand, it has confirmed the results of contemporary research into collegians' attitudes and values. More and more students are coming to college with their values already quite fixed; the colleges are having less and less impact on student values. The church is seen by much of college youth rather as a resource than as an authority in their lives. Many Catholic collegians pay little regard to the moral teaching of the official church, especially where sex is at issue. Many declare themselves Catholic while rejecting any obligation to "go to church" unless they feel like going.

On the other hand, I am ceaselessly moved, thrilled, humbled by the profound spirituality and social concern of many Georgetown students, and this in the midst of a pleasure-loving culture and a drug-addicted, so-called "mercenary" generation. Many have an intense prayer life, know and love Jesus as a real person, joy in genuine liturgy, even react excitedly to a well-orchestrated homily. As I indicated earlier, hundreds move out to the poor and downtrodden, the helpless and hopeless, from Fourteenth Street in Washington through Appalachia to Central America and beyond.

Just before graduation some years ago, a gifted, attractive, high-spirited senior told a largely adult worshiping community on the Hilltop: "Georgetown has opened my eyes to the rest of the world. I feel an obligation to give something of what I've been given." Several months later she was off to India, on funds she had begged, to share her nursing competence and her Christian compassion with the poor and the sick.

A final reason for optimism. A number of college presidents, members of Campus Compact: The Project for Public and Community Service (120 colleges and universities), met recently in the District of Columbia to issue a call for the promotion of public service "as a vital part of an undergraduate education." They are convinced "not only that young people can be led into increased public service but that they are not the money-grubbing materialists they are painted as being in the first place." Because they believe that youthful idealism needs only to be encouraged and channeled, these presidents trumpeted a resounding challenge to their presidential counterparts across America. Specifically, five challenges:

(1) Build a campus environment in which the service ethic is an integral part of the undergraduate experience;
(2) Work with federal, state and local government officials to establish programs that promote community service;
(3) Join in such national efforts as adult literacy and programs for disadvantaged children;
(4) Elicit the advice and support of faculty in order to make community service an ordinary part of campus life; and
(5) Promote awareness of civic involvement on their campuses.

The three co-chairs of Campus Compact? Howard Swearer, president of Brown; Donald Kennedy, president of Stanford; and Timothy Healy, president of Georgetown.[29]

A splendid Protestant preacher once said: the religious man or woman is "a queer mixture" of three persons, "the poet, the lunatic, the lover."[30] Such is my strange prayer for you for the days and years that lie ahead. I pray that the poet may always find a place in you; for the poet is a person of profound faith, seeing beneath the appearances of things, seeing with new eyes—in your case, with the eyes of Christ. I pray that there may ever be a fair measure of lunacy in you: the wild idea, the foolishness of the cross, the mad exchange of all else for God; for herein lies your Christian hope. And I pray that however radical the risk, however many the Judases who betray you, even on your cross you will always be Christ the lover, arms extended to your little world for its redemption—and yours.

With this hope and this prayer I end this essay in observation, in theology, and in prophecy, confident that the few "fat cats" whom the law of averages uncovers in any large group will be swallowed up by the greater number of you who, after the fashion of Christ, will be "suffering servants."[31]

Notes

1. Philip Rieff, *Freud: The Mind of the Moralist* (Garden City, N.Y.: Doubleday Anchor Books, 1961), 391.

2. Ibid., 390.

3. Ibid., 65.

4. Ibid., 361-62.

5. Robert N. Bellah, "Religion & Power in America Today," *Commonweal* 109, no. 21 (3 Dec. 1982): 650-55, at 652. I have not found it feasible, given the focus of my essay, to include Bellah's remarks on the ideal of psychological man/woman, who "pushes the logic of economic man one stage further" (651).

6. See *Time* 128, no. 10 (8 Sept. 1986): 57.

7. See William Raspberry, "'A Rising Tide of Materialism'," *Washington Post,* 1 Feb. 1988, A15.

8. Ibid. Not having seen the actual report, I am dependent on Raspberry's column, quoting not only his remarks but his quotations as well.

9. Ibid.

10. *Esquire,* February 1988, 79-90.

11. Ibid., 79-80.

12. Andrew Greeley, "A Post-Vatican II New Breed?," *America* 144, no. 25 (27 June 1981): 537.

13. In this second section I am borrowing liberally from a chapter, "Let Justice Roll Down Like Waters," in my *Preaching: The Art and the Craft* (New York/ Mahwah: Paulist, c1987), 119-38, specifically 120-27. I have updated some of the material.

14. George G. Higgins, "The Church and Social Concerns," syndicated column, excerpted from *One Voice* (Diocese of Birmingham, Ala.), 27 April 1979, 4.

15. Pius XII, *Allocutio ad cultores historiae et artis,* 9 May 1956 (*AAS* 48 [1956] 212).

16. *Decree on the Apostolate of the Laity,* no. 5; see also no. 7. In response to this quotation, one might dredge up the affirmation in the Council's *Pastoral Constitu-*

tion on the Church in the Modern World, no. 42: "Christ, to be sure, gave his Church no proper mission in the political, economic, or social order. The purpose which he set before it is a religious one. . . . " Here the crucial Latin terms are "missio propria" and "finis . . . ordinis religiosi." Discussion of these phrases is not possible here, but two observations seem to be in order. (1) The passage just quoted is not excluding the Christian community from playing a significant, transforming role in the social, economic, and political orders. Such an interpretation would make nonsense out of Part 1, chapter 4. The text reaffirms the legitimate autonomy that belongs to the temporal order. For the historical background of this chapter (nos. 40-45) and an insightful presentation of its meaning, see Yves Congar's chapter, "The Role of the Church in the Modern World," in Herbert Vorgrimler, ed., *Commentary on the Documents of Vatican II,* vol. 5 (New York: Herder and Herder, 1969), 202-23. E.g., "The Church's function comprises everything human. . . . Consequently the Church must not be restricted to a 'religious' domain, identical in practice with public worship" (213). (2) There is a problem on what "church" means in chapter 4. Charles Moeller argues, from the proposed amendments, that whereas in chapters 1-3 it means "the People of God," in chapter 4 it refers to the hierarchy (ibid., 61-62). Congar (ibid., 211 and 214 [see no. 28 for pertinent *relatio*]), without alluding to Moeller's position, says the church in chapter 4 is "the People of God," "the social body." The difference in interpretation of "church" is obviously not irrelevant to one's understanding of the church's mission.

17. 1971 Synod of Bishops, *De iustitia in mundo* (Vatican Press, 1971), Introduction, p. 5. One may argue whether "constitutive" in the document means "integral" or "essential." The 1976 document of the International Theological Commission, "Human Development & Christian Salvation," trans. Walter J. Burghardt, S.J., *Origins* 7, no. 20 (3 Nov. 1977): 311, states that "it seems more accurate to interpret [*ratio constitutiva*] as meaning an integral part, not an essential part" (IV). That interpretation is discussable. What is beyond argument is that the Synod saw the search for justice as inseparable from the preaching of the gospel.

18. 1974 Synod of Bishops, "Human Rights and Reconciliation," *Origins* 4 (1974): 318.

19. "Human Development & Christian Salvation" IV (trans. *Origins* [n. 17 above]: 310-11).

20. John Paul II, *Sollicitudo rei socialis* (Encyclical on Social Concerns), nos. 21 and 22 (Vatican English-language text, *Origins* 17, no. 38 [March 3, 1988]: 648).

21. For a careful appraisal of "what the Old and New Testaments have to say about the relationship between salvation and human welfare, between salvation and human rights," see the document of the International Theological Commission (n. 17 above), III (trans. *Origins,* 309-10). See also Franz Böckle, ed., *The Social Message of the Gospels* (Concilium 35; New York: Paulist, 1968).

22. On the potential "misuse" of Mt 25:31-46 in contemporary ethics and proclamation, and for an effort to highlight some of the more significant challenges of the parable, see John R. Donahue, S.J., "The 'Parable' of the Sheep and the Goats: A Challenge to Christian Ethics," *Theological Studies* 47 (1986): 3-31.

23. Address of Pope John Paul II opening the deliberations of the Third Assembly of Latin American Bishops, Puebla, 28 Jan. 1979, III, 2. An English translation is available in *Origins* 8, no. 34 (8 Feb. 1979): 530-38; but I have not used it for the passage quoted, because it translates *indispensable* as "essential" (536), apparently unaware of the problem to which I allude in n. 17 above. I take it that the pope and/or his speechwriter consciously avoided a philosophical interpretation of the 1971 Synod's *ratio constitutiva;* it is enough that a facet of the church's evangelizing mission be described as something which the church may not refuse to do; it is not capable of being dispensed with; the church cannot be released from this obligation. The pope goes on to cite Paul VI's *Evangelii nuntiandi,* 29: "evangelization would not be complete if it did not take into account the unceasing interplay of the Gospel and of man's concrete life, both personal and social" (trans. *Origins,* 536).

24. National Conference of Catholic Bishops, *The Challenge of Peace: God's Promise and Our Response* (Washington, D.C.: United States Catholic Conference, 1983).

25. National Conference of Catholic Bishops, *Economic Justice for All: Catholic Social Teaching and the U.S. Economy* (Washington, D.C.: United States Catholic Conference, 1986).

26. Cf., e.g., David Hollenbach, S.J., "Whither Nuclear Deterrence? The Moral Debate Continues," *Theological Studies* 47 (1986): 117-33; John Langan, S.J., "The Pastoral on the Economy: From Drafts to Policy," ibid., 48 (1987): 135-56; both have extensive bibliographical references and discuss some of the more crucial issues.

27. From the statement issued by the Catholic Bishops' Conference of the Philippines, after an emergency meeting in the week following the February 7 national elections; text in *Asian Focus,* 21 Feb. 1986, 8. My quotations from Cardinal Sin's talk are taken from a text delivered to Georgetown University by Sin and made available by the university in duplicated form.

28. Robert N. Bellah, "Religion & Power in America Today," *Commonweal* 109, no. 21 (3 Dec. 1982): 650-55, at 655.

29. My information on Campus Compact and my quotations are drawn from a column by William Raspberry, "Not All Students Are Greedy," *Washington Post,* 3 Feb. 1988, A19.

30. See Frederick Buechner, *The Magnificent Defeat* (New York: Seabury, 1966), 23.

31. I should note that there is not an irreconcilable opposition between "fat cats" and "suffering servants." Money, power, and reputation are not ethical evils—not in themselves. Like so much else, they take their morality or im-

morality from a single-syllable question: Why? Are these ends or means? And if means, means to what? Money, however hard-earned, is a gift from the very God who made it all possible by giving life and breath, talent and toughness; a gift not to be clutched in hot little hands but to be given, to be shared, to lift the less-gifted from the grime and grit, to slake their hunger for bread or justice, for peace or freedom, for knowledge or understanding, even for God. Power is a possession plagued with peril but potent with promise. Not because it satisfies a lust for control, but because it lets one be a servant, minister to sisters and brothers, imitate the God and Father of us all, whose power is identical with his love, his goodness, his self-giving. Reputation is not ours to ape Narcissus, the mythological youth who fell in love with his own image. Fame allows the other to know us, to know what we are like, and so to lie at our golden gate, like poor Lazarus in the gospel, and be fed at least with the crumbs from our table (cf. Lk 16:20-21).

Vincent O'Keefe, S.J.

Jesuit Education: Myth and Reality, Context and Mission

Vincent O'Keefe, S.J., is Vice President for Special Projects at the Jesuit Conference in Washington, D.C.

I. Myth

Myths, like heroes, play a great role in our lives. In fact, life would be terribly impoverished without them. An unfortunate tendency to equate myth with fiction does a real injustice to a literary form that served to expound a truth or its origins.

Unfortunately, today myths have a way of being telescoped or concretized in a maxim or a pithy saying which can degenerate into a slogan. "Remember the Alamo" can mean very different things to different people. I received a birthday card with "Remember the Alamo" on the first page. Inside was the crusher: "You would!"

Rome is a great place for choice sayings: "*Roma veduta, fede perduta*" is one. That comes out as: "See Rome and lose your faith." Another one is: "In Rome everything is a mystery, but nothing is secret."

One of the banners in a recent St. Patrick's Day parade in New York carried the motto of the famous 69th Regiment: "Gentle if stroked; fierce if provoked." It seems to me that the President of Georgetown University had some ties to that regiment.

When we turn to education, we are all familiar with "You can always tell a Harvard man." To which the inevitable wag adds: "But not much!"

A favorite and frequently heard maxim to sum up Jesuit education is "The Jesuits taught me how to think." A cursory glance at some of those who were turned out by Jesuit institutions—and I mean that "turned out" in every sense—will show the formula can take on different meanings on the lips of different people. Much depends on whether it is a Voltaire or a Cardinal Spellman; Fidel Castro or General de Gaulle; William Bennett or Timothy Healy; Alfred Hitchcock or Bing Crosby; Patrick Buchanan or Patrick Ewing. All of the above were, of course, turned out by Jesuit institutions.

One finds this focus on "learning how to think" as *the* note of Jesuit education in some interesting contexts. Last summer in the middle of a body-and-soul numbing fourteen-hour nonstop flight, I was watching a movie called "Glitter Dome," based on a novel by Joseph Wambaugh. This sparkling bit of dialogue caught my fading attention: "The Jesuits did a helluva job on Marty. He liked to chalk it on the board, showing all the links."

Of course, we are all for learning how to think, and it is great as far as it goes. But there's the rub. It does not go far enough. It centers more on the slogan than on the fuller content and truth of the myth.

"Learning how to think" tends to reduce Jesuit education to a purely cognitive activity, as though the centerpiece of the whole process would be ratiocination, pure and unadulterated reasoning, and as though the ideal graduate would be a cool, detached and uninvolved ratiocinator—and probably terminally dull as well. It has the sound of a disembodied intellect, steeped not so much in philosophy as in minor logic. The magic formula would consist of two parts *Ratio Studiorum* and one part iron discipline. It would turn out a scholastic Sherlock Holmes.

You may smile at the mention of Sherlock Holmes—and your imagination, like mine, may project the face of Basil Rathbone—but 1987 marked the centenary of the appearance of Sherlock Holmes, and to my point the full name of his creator was Sir Arthur *Ignatius* Conan Doyle. The Ignatius was for Ignatius Loyola, our Jesuit founder. Doyle was educated at the famous British Jesuit institution, Stonyhurst College. It also seems that the architecture of Baskerville Hall was modeled on Stonyhurst. In his later years, Doyle dropped the name along with many other things related to it, but that is another tale.

In summation, there is indeed a myth surrounding Jesuit education. My quarrel is not with the idea of myth because this can help us to understand certain realities in an engaging and imaginative way. When the myth degenerates into a pat saying or slogan, then the reality is in danger of being distorted to the point of parody or falsification.

II. Reality

When we turn to the reality of Jesuit education, we must confess how indebted we all are to Brian Daley, S.J. for his extraordinary opening lecture: "Splendor and Wonder: Ignatian Mysticism and the Ideals of Liberal Education." His lecture showed the intimate relation between Jesuit education and the *Spiritual Exercises* of St. Ignatius, "a deep correspondence, an inner affinity, between the Christian pedogogy or mystagogy of the *Spiritual Exercises,* that great vehicle for communicating the Jesuit spirit, and the effect on the human person of liberal studies at their best."[1]

The reality of Jesuit education, like every other Jesuit work, is based on

Jesuit inspiration, spirit and heritage. All authentic Jesuit spirit flows from the *Spiritual Exercises,* which gave birth to the Society of Jesus, to its life and work. They are our Jesuit roots, our places in the heart, our heart and soul. In and through the *Exercises,* Jesuits are able to renew their faith and hope by experiencing again the love of God. This same spiritual experience enables and teaches us how to maintain the freedom and objectivity we need for a continuing review and renewal of our work.

Jesuit education is centered in a spirit that is embodied in a set of characteristics, and these characteristics help us to identify Jesuit education.

III. Characteristics

From the *Spiritual Exercises* we draw a view of the person which orients and enlivens our educational process. Through the *Exercises* we are helped to understand our origin and our nature and end as well as the end of all human society. We view all women and men as coming from God, as made in God's image and likeness, and therefore intelligent and free and equal. This situates our view of the true dignity of the individual person, and the central place in all our lives and in all history of Jesus Christ. This central part of our spirit and heritage we bring to our endeavors in education. That is why we speak of a Christian humanism that seeks to provide an integral view of human existence, not a partial or distorted or cheapened view.

For this reason, a characteristic of Jesuit education is a full-blown concern to develop intellectual probity, critical intelligence, and responsible freedom.

Reason holds a prominent place in Jesuit education and must be given its due, especially since distrust of reason is unfortunately a recurring phenomenon in many shapes and forms, particularly in the wake of gross oversimplification and slogans.

We look to an enquiring mind because we are dealing with true education and not just training. We try to probe our human condition while recognizing our true human worth. There is a thrust against narrowness of mind, against our tendency to absolutize our own experience and reactions. We look to develop a sense of historical perspective which helps to de-provincialize our outlook. The advancement of truth is God's work, and a prime way of helping others is to help them humanize their intelligence.

With a view to this humanization, our educational heritage sets high value on developing the imagination, helping students to be literate and widely read, and including a devotion to the dramatic arts. Many are surprised to find the quality and quantity of theatrical representations in Jesuit institutions. But this belongs to our early Jesuit tradition. When the Society of Jesus was suppressed in 1773, there were fifty-three Jesuit theaters in Poland alone.

Jesuit dramas were so influential that in the seventeenth and early eighteenth centuries they were a link between drama and opera. The ballet, too, played a great part in the Jesuit educational enterprise. The aim was not purely didactic or moralistic; it was humanistic and cultural, a part of a continual effort to turn out well-rounded human beings.

In a word, a critical intelligence will be tough-minded and open-minded, with a sense of historical perspective, leaving plenty of play for the imagination in striving to be articulate in expressing one's views and convictions.

IV. Moral Sensitivity

In Jesuit education there is a concern to develop moral sensitivity and a concern with ultimate questions. Along with an intellectual and cultural climate there must be a moral ambience where values are present and discussed gracefully and profoundly. The concern is not just for what works, but for what matters. Hence there is a concern with philosophical and theological issues and questions. Moral sensitivity helps one to see through and beyond passing fads and catchy slogans, helps to develop a sense of moral judgment which goes beyond mere likes and dislikes.

A concern with ultimate questions, those dealing with life and death issues, does not mean these issues are the monopoly of philosophy and theology. As we know, literature and drama, to cite but two examples, are a privileged field and locus for meeting and dealing with such questions.

We know all too well that education does not automatically humanize people; the intellectually proficient person can be morally bankrupt. Our educational process fails if it produces a trained expert who lacks a moral sense and concern, who has no commitment to any values that go beyond the here-and-now, or that look beyond self-interest and self-fulfillment.

Since its inception, the Society of Jesus was intended as a group of men at the service of the church and the human family. Ignatius wanted his men to be free to serve anywhere in the world and in whatever capacity for the greater glory of God. To assure this universal spirit he linked his group by a special bond of service and love to the Roman Pontiff, whose care extends to the universal church. Ignatius wanted this universal spirit to be a part of the Society of Jesus, of its life and work. Once he realized the critical importance of education, he promoted it as an apostolic work for his order. Jesuit schools grew and spread rapidly wherever Jesuits were to be found. The form and shape of these institutions were gradually adapted to the local situation, but the essentials of the Jesuit spirit and heritage were maintained. Rooted in the church's tradition, the Jesuit spirit and heritage in education evoke a universal spirit. The context of Jesuit education in today's American Jesuit college and university must include this universal spirit. It means our educational process should look to all cultures and races, and to all areas of human concern. It entails a respect for complexity and pluralism and for differences of opinion. It includes a concern for civility and civil discourse and sweet reasonableness, and an aversion to prejudice and narrowness of mind and spirit. This has a particular application in the study of religion.

Theology as a university discipline is not the same as faith or spirituality or holiness. The university is not the place for indoctrination. In the Jesuit educational process there is a concern to provide the students with a good knowledge of the Catholic theological heritage, and to help them consider the religious dimensions of the major issues in contemporary culture and society. Theology studies are meant to enable the student to think and act within a vision of life that includes religious values. An educational process that omits religious values is an incomplete and deformed process. When we speak of the light of the gospel and of gospel values, this does not mean an automatic serving up of solutions to problems. It is rather meant as furnishing a guiding light for the purpose of expanding human insight.

V. An Historical Perspective

In dealing with any Catholic institution of higher education, Georgetown included, it is essential to place things in their proper historical perspective. The university has a very long history, and both its beginnings and its development can help one understand certain things that gained a fixed place in the university. John W. Donohue, S.J., a leading expert on Jesuit education, has explained the origins of the university's penchant for independence this way:

> If the terminology weren't anachronistic, one could say that the university is a secular institution invented by a Christian civilization. The inventors wouldn't have put it that way, however, because in the High Middle Ages religion was so intermingled with temporal affairs as to make the concept of the secular hard to grasp clearly. In St. Thomas Aquinas' day, the Church kept usurious bankers under some control, just as in the Massachusetts Bay Colony the Puritans set price ceilings on rare goods like nails. Since neither of these societies had fully developed secular agencies for dealing with politics, business, education, welfare and the arts, the Church took up the slack. That had practical benefits, but did cloud the distinction between religion, the sphere of one's relationship to God, and the secular, the sphere of one's relationship to one's natural and social environments.
>
> Still, the distinction was at least partly perceived especially by the embryonic universities, even though all their personnel were clerics. In the histories of Paris and Oxford, for instance, certain broad lines of development can be traced. Those communities of masters and students saw themselves as a third force not to be identified either with civil society on the one hand or the Church on the other. If their chief business was the higher learning, their chief extra-curricular problem was maintaining enough autonomy to keep the *studium* from becoming the vassal either of the *imperium* or the *sacerdotium.* To do this, they played those powers off against one another. They got papal bulls to endow them with the character of moral persons charged with conduct of their own affairs, and then urged their immunities whenever kings, bishops or tavern keepers tried to dictate. At the same time, the universities kept their guard up lest the Pope's influence diminish what we would call their academic freedom.
>
> That freedom had its hazards, of course, at all levels of university life. It reluctantly sheltered the enormous student appetite for brawling, lechery, and such irreverences as dicing on the altars of Notre Dame after holiday revels. More significantly, it provided the masters with opportunities to develop their thinking freely, and this meant that, rightly or wrongly, medieval faculties were often charged with heresy. In one extraordinary burst of enthusiasm in 1277, the Bishop of Paris and the Archbishop of Canterbury both censured some opinions of St. Thomas, who had died only three years before. All those ancient scufflings have faded from the collective consciousness of the West, but not without first having established the principle that the university by its very nature is neither a church nor a department of state, and ought not be bullied by either.[2]

Needless to say, the University of Paris has a special place in the history of the Society of Jesus. Ignatius and his first group of nine associates who banded together to form the Society, all studied together at the University of Paris. Ignatius gained his Master's degree in Arts before beginning his theological studies, and was commonly addressed as "Maître Ignace."

VI. Knowledge for Service

"Knowledge is power" has become a current and accepted expression in our day. For Ignatius and for Jesuit education, however, knowledge is linked not so much with power as with service. The Jesuit institution puts itself at the service of the human family. It reaches out and is involved in the local scene. There is no fortress mentality, but rather a concern for the pressing contemporary issues of our human society, like true peace and justice, poverty and violence, the family and genetic research, and illiteracy, just to name a few.

The Jesuit college and university endeavor to shed light on the mystery of life and to cooperate, as only they can, in helping to find some answers to the critical problems of our times.

VII. The Mission of Jesuit Education

It is well known that the present pope, John Paul II, has spoken to the Society of Jesus on what he expects of its members.

In an address to the provincials and central government of the Society of Jesus in 1982, he said: "As my venerated predecessor, Pope Paul VI, already told you, the Church today wants the Society to implement the Second Vatican Council, as in the time of St. Ignatius and afterwards. It spared no effort to make known and apply the Council of Trent, assisting in a notable way the Roman Pontiffs in the exercise of their supreme magisterium."[3]

John Paul II repeats what Paul VI had said:

> [Members of the Society] are in the first line of the profound renewal which the Church, especially since the Second Vatican Council, desires to bring about in the secularized world. Your Society is, so to speak, a test of the Church's vitality throughout the centuries; it is in some sense a crossroads where, in a very significant manner, difficulties, temptations, efforts, undertakings, the durability and the successes of the entire Church all meet together.[4]

When the Holy Father specifies more concretely what the church expects of the Society of Jesus, the program includes the following: to help the pope implement the Second Vatican Council; to adapt traditional Jesuit apostolates toward this end; to work toward the Christian penetration of the culture of the surrounding world; to exercise pastoral care of those on the fringe of society; to exercise the priestly ministry in all its authentic forms; to adapt Jesuit apostolic work to the demands and opportunities of a new world of communication; to promote ecumenism, the deepening of relations with non-Christian religions and with nonbelievers, while resisting atheism; and to promote justice in the church's evangelizing action.

That, I submit, constitutes a tremendous mandate. It is no small-minded, confining and parochial program, but is one based on a vision of the world and the church that is far-reaching and profound, and challenges us to find the people, competent and committed, to face up to it.

The Second Vatican Council was the first major official event in which the church realized its status precisely as a world church in action. It marked the transition of the Western church to a world church. It also marked a change from a culturally monocentric church, predominantly European and North American, to a culturally polycentric world church.

When John Paul II asked the Society of Jesus to help him and the bishops implement the genuine spirit of Vatican II in serving the church, he intended service in this world church. This change means working for a strong and dynamic unity while preserving legitimate differences. It means serving the church in dialogue with and at the service of the human family.

I would like to focus on one of the points indicated by the Holy Father, namely, "the Christian penetration of the culture of the world around us."[5] I do this because we are dealing here with something of great importance in the eyes of the pope, as will become clear in what follows.

On May 20, 1982 John Paul II instituted the Pontifical Council for Culture. This council is a special permanent body for the purpose of promoting the great objectives which the Second Vatican Council proposed regarding the relations between the church and culture. It is meant to give the whole church a common impulse in the continuously renewed encounter between the salvific message of the gospel and the multiplicity of cultures.

"Since the beginning of my pontificate," says the pope, "I have considered the Church's dialogue with cultures of our time to be a vital area, one in which the destiny of the world at the end of this 20th century is at stake. Now people live a fully human life thanks to culture. Yes, the future of people depends on culture."[6]

What does the word "culture" mean for us? What image does it evoke? Music and opera, painting and sculpture and museums? Pop culture? Literature? *Gaudium et Spes* enlightens us by spelling out the broad sense in which we are to understand culture and cultures. It says:

> The word "culture" in its general sense indicates all those factors by which man refines and unfolds his manifold spiritual and bodily qualities. It means the effort to bring the world itself under his control by his knowledge and labor. It includes the fact that by improving customs and institutions he renders social life more human both within the family and in the civic community. Finally, it is a feature of culture that throughout the course of time man expresses, communicates, and conserves in his works great spiritual experiences and desires, so that these may be of advantage to the progress of many, even of the whole human family.[7]

Paul VI had prepared the way. "The split," he had said, "between the Gospel and culture is without a doubt the drama of our time. Therefore, every effort must be made to ensure a full evangelization of culture, or more correctly, of cultures."[8]

He also said: "For the Church it is a question of affecting and as it were upsetting, through the power of the Gospel, mankind's criteria of judgment, determining values, points of interest, lines of thought, sources of inspiration and models of life, which are in contrast with the Word of God and the plan of salvation."[9]

John Paul II follows in the same vein as he tells us:

> There is an organic and constitutive link existing between Christianity and culture—with man, therefore. And if culture is that by which man as man becomes more man, what is at stake here is the very destiny of man. The synthesis between faith and culture is not just a demand of culture but also of faith. A faith which does not become culture is a faith which has not been fully received, nor thoroughly thought through, nor faithfully lived out.[10]

That brief phrase in the pope's address to the Society of Jesus, "to work toward the Christian penetration of the culture of the world around us," is seen in its full dimensions as a whole program, and even a way of life, of critical importance. We are dealing here with the principles and values which make up the ethos of a people, those things which underpin our criteria for judging and setting goals and priorities, the attitudes, customs models, laws and structures of the society in which we live. Who determines this composite of principles and values, and who articulates it, whether it be the popular thing to do or not, and how is this done? These questions bring us to the role and mission of Georgetown University in the area of culture.

Since the Second Vatican Council there has been a heightened sense of both the need for and the possibility of shaping a more truly human culture. It has also become increasingly clear that Catholic universities like Georgetown are playing a critical role in the shaping of this culture.

In our contemporary society, where almost anything is possible technologically, a tremendous and concentrated effort is needed for all the study, analysis, evaluation, expertise and action that will go into the shaping of our culture and our future. We surely need men and women who know how to evaluate and deal with technologies that determine the values and priorities of our society, and how to deal with the effects of these technologies on our economic and social goals, on communication networks, on our philosophies and our way of life.

In our educational process, as in life itself, so much depends on how we view the human person, our human society, our goals and our end in life. Shaping a truly human culture in our society involves a quest for a humanism that gives first place to the values of human dignity and worth, of fraternity and justice, while correcting and "re-dimensioning" those values in our world which reduce the meaning of life chiefly to the many different material and economic factors.

Georgetown's heritage and tradition leads it to promote a culture in its educational programs and life that emphasizes the values of human dignity and the good life in its fullest sense. The quest is to develop the totally human person through the humanities, sciences, professional courses and all the activities that are a part of university life in a Catholic institution. There is also a particular perspective on the ultimate nature and destiny of women and men which is part of Georgetown's tradition. This is spelled out in a respect for religious experiences and for religious questions which are viewed as central to human life. And the humanism which Georgetown espouses is helped and strengthened, rather than weakened or diluted, by a religious commitment. There is a firm and assured place for educational values that have their origins in religious experiences and convictions, which can appeal to others who may not necessarily share these experiences and convictions. Georgetown's tradition also underlines strongly a method of teaching that is highly personal, which seeks the full personal development of the student and believes in a close personal relationship between teacher and student. Since the heritage and tradition is a sound and living one, Georgetown's educational process can be imaginative and creative in facing different situations and new challenges.

The role, then, of Georgetown in this area of shaping our contemporary culture is a major one. With her sister institutions, she makes an essential and unique contribution to society by embodying in her educational process a probing and profound study of our crucial human problems and concerns. This is a study far removed from the facile and superficial world of slogans, of purely emotional and self-centered responses, and of instant, simplistic solutions. Teaching and research and all that goes into the educational process are of the highest importance at Georgetown because they reject and refute any partial or deformed vision of the person. This is in sharp contrast to so many current approaches which lead to a minimizing or cheapening or threatening of the human person. Georgetown can focus its different disciplines on the central issues of our society in an interdisciplinary approach that can be found only in a university. In this way, men and women are being prepared for the constructive criticism and evaluation of our culture that a healthy society needs, women and men who are learning not only ways to make a living, but also how to make a life that is worth living. The main issues facing our society involve complex, empirical factors: genetic research, abortion, and care of the dying, for example, in an age of revolution in medical technology; economic justice and civil rights, for example, on the national scene; nuclear warfare and human rights, for example, on the world scene. But all these issues also have a moral dimension and they cannot be defined, discussed or decided without important moral choices. Georgetown's role is to shape and sharpen our culture by shaping and sharpening the issues of intellect and conscience that face our society.

For the church of Vatican II that goes to meet and dialogue with the world and its culture, Georgetown's educational process provides an ideal location for this in Christian witness, in scientific and theological inquiry, and in cultural synthesis.

And Georgetown does this, not as a parish or a seminary would, but precisely as a university following its heritage and tradition. This heritage and tradition promotes a culture that emphasizes the values of human dignity and the good life in its fullest sense by fostering academic excellence and moral responsibility and sensitivity, and by treating religious experiences and questions as central to our culture and life. The aim here is that of Ignatius Loyola: the greater good.

Notes

1. p. 16.
2. Cf. John W. Donohue, S.J., "Catholic Universities Define Themselves: A Progress Report," *America* (April 21, 1973): 356.
3. "Allocution of Pope John Paul II to Jesuit Provincial Superiors, Feb. 27, 1982" in *Conventus Provincialium Societatis Iesu,* published by the Generalate of the Society of Jesus (Rome, 1982), 36.
4. Ibid.
5. Loc. cit., 38.
6. "Allocution to Cardinals," in *L'Osservatore Romano,* 10 Nov. 1979.
7. *Gaudium et Spes,* n. 53, in *The Documents of Vatican II,* Walter M. Abbott, S.J., ed. (New York: America Press, 1962), 259.
8. *Evangelii Nuntiandi,* n. 20, in *On Evangelization in the Modern World* (Washington, D.C.: United States Catholic Conference, 1976).
9. Op. cit., n. 19.
10. "Letter to Cardinal Agostino Casaroli, Secretary of State, May 20, 1982," in *L'Osservatore Romano,* 21-22 May 1982.

JAMES A. DEVEREUX, S.J.

The Challenge of Georgetown to the Society of Jesus

JAMES A. DEVEREUX, S.J., is Provincial of the Maryland Province of the Society of Jesus and former member of the English Department at Georgetown University.

It is customary for a speaker to begin by telling his gentle listeners how happy he is to be with them—customary but not invariably true. This evening I can honor both custom and truth. I am delighted to be at Georgetown University and to speak to you in this series of lectures on the Jesuits and the Georgetown spirit. So many of you are friends and former colleagues. My four-and-a-half years at this university, though sometimes arduous, were truly happy.

The cause of my delight this evening is at once particular and universal. It is a joy to be here both because Georgetown is Georgetown—a unique institution that I know and love—and because Georgetown is a university. To a man of ruminative temper with some sympathy for young people, a university is the place to be. What a piece of work is a university! How noble in reason, how infinite in faculties! The alteration of the text does some violence to its prose rhythm, but I think that Hamlet would agree to it by way of experiment. He was, after all, a Wittenberg man.

And surely a university is a noble piece of work, one that stands among the most splendid achievements of civilization. Is there any other institution which directs us toward the mysteries of past, present and future, and invites us to explore them as far as the human mind will lead and to pass on our discoveries to the rising generation?

I am happy, then, to be here tonight because this is Georgetown and because it is a university. But I have still another reason to be pleased, and that is because I come here as a Jesuit. I would contend that there is a special affinity between Jesuits and universities. As institutions they offer the members of the Society of Jesus a way to be and to act as Jesuits in the fullest sense. Indeed, I believe that this university, Georgetown, presents the Society of Jesus a unique opportunity to carry out its purposes as a religious order. Perhaps I should rather say a challenge, which is an opportunity that entails risks. This evening, then, I wish to speak to you about the challenge that Georgetown offers the Society of Jesus.

The association of the Jesuits with universities was not an immediate phenomenon historically, nor was it, I suppose, metaphysically necessary. We think of a university as a gathering of persons and resources to explore and expand human knowledge and to share it with rising generations. In itself it is a secular institution, a quintessential distillation of human culture. The Society of Jesus, on the other hand, is a Roman Catholic religious order whose aims are supernatural and apostolic. A good Jesuit always has an ulterior motive. He is on a mission given him by the Church: to advance in some way or another the reign of God on earth and thus to promote his greater glory. In the view of the Society's founder, Ignatius of Loyola, a Jesuit may do this in any one of a score of ways: by preaching the word, by directing others in the Spiritual Exercises, by administering the sacraments, by feeding the hungry, by teaching little children. Although they were in fact university-trained men, the first companions of Ignatius did not set about at once to teach in universities. Soon enough, though, Ignatius turned to formal education as an apostolate. The Jesuits did begin to teach in universities and establish new ones, among them Georgetown.

John Carroll's College on the Potomac began modestly enough as a school for boys, but eventually it grew into a full-fledged university, "branchy between towers," with thousands of students, a learned faculty and a distinct identity of its own. And the Society of Jesus, which was present at its birth, has stayed with the institution these almost two hundred years. Why do we Jesuits stay here? Ours is supposed to be a mobile religious order. Is it simply inertia, or have we been seduced by the human attractions of university life? These explanations cannot be ruled out a priori, but I don't think that they suffice. The reason why we are here and why we intend to stay is that Georgetown offers the Society of Jesus a unique context in which to pursue its apostolic mission, and one that is in harmony with the purposes of this university. That lyre on Georgetown's seal of which Father Ron Murphy spoke so eloquently earlier in this series symbolizes a complex but attainable harmony of purposes toward which both the order and the university aspire.

Before I become too lyrical, let me first speak of a number of concrete circumstances which make such a common pursuit possible and which help make Georgetown such an attractive field of labor for the Society of Jesus. Among them is the never-to-be-sneezed-at fact that the institution is solvent. It is able to provide its students and faculty with facilities and services to carry out its educational work. Its financial stability also makes it possible for Georgetown to open its doors to students who could not otherwise afford to enter them. Although its endowment is small by comparison with other institutions of similar importance, that endowment has grown exponentially in the last decade and gives promise of continued growth. The university also enjoys the strong support of its alumni. It is true that black ink, bricks and mortar do not a university make, but one cannot make a university without them.

Far more important, Georgetown now enjoys the most learned lay and Jesuit faculty that it has had in two hundred years. I realize that statement cannot be proven, but I would stake my life on it, or at least my sacred honor. Moreover, the university is now able to attract among the best scholars in the land, so that the quality of its faculty, which is the ultimate gauge of a university's excellence, will surely continue to grow. As for Georgetown's students, anyone who has had the pleasure of teaching them knows that they are intelligent, energetic—indeed, fairly driven. Yet despite that, many are still quite susceptible to the seductions of idealism, both intellectual, moral and religious. Partly by design and partly by necessity, the university has resisted the temptation to become all things to all people, and has focused on certain areas of knowledge and instruction, among them law and history, medicine, the art of government, philosophy, languages, literature and, of course, theology. Finally, Georgetown enjoys the leadership of a president who has been able to articulate brilliantly for the university community and the country as a whole what Georgetown is and would wish to be. Unlike many universities elsewhere in the world, Georgetown, along with the other private institutions of higher learning in this country, is able to pursue its educational purposes relatively free of government interference, while still enjoying not insubstantial government support.

I have been speaking of a number of happy circumstances which the Society of Jesus discovers at this moment at Georgetown, circumstances which help to make the Society's encounter with the university an opportunity that is full of promise. What do the Jesuits bring to this encounter? They bring a group of 57 men who are active in the university: 39 as teachers, 7 in various kinds of pastoral care, and 11 as administrators. As professional men, they are competent in their fields. Many are exceptionally fine teachers, a few are distinguished scholars. They live in common and are closely bound by religious vows, by friendship and by dedication to a work in which they believe. The Jesuit community constitutes a corporation legally distinct from the university. The community does not own Georgetown University. Jesuit teachers and administrators constitute less than five percent of the full-time faculty. Whatever the myth, the university is not run from the Jesuit recreation room. For that matter,

I don't believe that any great university is run by a person or a group of persons in the way a corporation is. It may be nudged and cajoled, and its faculty and administration can surely give it direction or fail to do so, but a university has a weight and a momentum of its own, and resists sudden change. In any case, the Jesuits are happy about Georgetown's present direction, and want to play a role in its future.

In addressing my topic this evening, "The Challenge of Georgetown to the Society of Jesus," I've tried to describe the Jesuit community that lives and works at Georgetown. If challenge first means opportunity, a chance for good, then what opportunity is offered the Jesuits at Georgetown? How can they contribute to the life of this institution in a way that is consonant with the community's own purposes?

In Shakespeare's play, King Lear cries out in desperation: "Who is it that can tell me who I am?" (1.4.230) To tell another who he is, is a precious, indeed a life-giving gift—as precious to institutions as it is to individuals. The Jesuit community at Georgetown, by what its members say and how they act, can tell the university who it is and ought to be. The community knows what kind of a place Georgetown is. I find it significant that Georgetown's formal history was written in the past and is being written today by Georgetown Jesuits. Besides historical knowledge, the members of the Jesuit community have a kind of folk memory of the university. As a group, they have identified wholeheartedly with the institution. Other universities have close structural ties with church bodies and religious traditions. What is unusual here is that Georgetown is tied to a concrete community with a distinct history that stretches back without interruption to the community first headed by John Carroll.

A number of years ago when I was rector of the Jesuit community at Georgetown, the question arose of moving our living quarters from the present location across from Dahlgren Chapel to new apartments some blocks away. The chief reason we decided against this move was symbolic. The Jesuit community belongs at the geographical and historic and spiritual heart of the university, not because it controls it or desires to do so, but because it is in touch with the idea of Georgetown and ought to be its special advocate within the larger university community.

What is this idea which gives Georgetown its identity as a university? Happily, that question has been answered with great skill and learning by my predecessors in this series. Father Brian Daley first traced Georgetown's ideal of liberal education to the mysticism of Ignatius of Loyola, and Father Ron Murphy showed how that ideal is implicit in the motto of the university's seal, *Utraque Unum.* St. Paul, referring to the Gentiles and the Jews, who until then had been separated, wrote to the Gentiles at Ephesus that Christ had made both peoples one—*utraque unum* (Eph 2:14). The founders of Georgetown took up this motto and understood it in a way that was applicable to the new college. Their desire from the beginning was to create an institution which would bring diverse elements into unity. The first prospectus for Georgetown College on the Potomac says that "the object of the proposed institution is to unite the means of communicating science with an effectual provision for guarding and preserving the morals of youth. With this view the Seminary will be superintended by those who, having had experience in similar institutions, know that an undivided attention may be given to the cultivation of virtue and to literary improvement." The institution was to aim at both the study of the arts and sciences and the living of a virtuous life, because the two are compatible.

The very same idea of harmony, of a coincidence of opposites, to use the Renaissance phrase, is found in the university's current prospectus entitled "The Educational Goals and Objectives of the Georgetown University Main Campus." There we read: "Georgetown, by virtue of its Catholic and Jesuit origins, has a rich and special view of reality, one that celebrates human dignity in a godly context." The Georgetown ideal of liberal education "aims at disclosing all that it means to be a human being: a center of consciousness and choice, immersed in a physical world and bound to other persons in human society, yet possessed of transcendent value because created and graced by God." The goals and objectives statement describes this viewpoint as "a soberly optimistic humanism [that] flows from Christianity. Catholic Christians, while recognizing the presence in the world of tragedy and conflict, see it as infused with the goodness of its Maker. . . . For this reason, [they] see no sector of human experience as beyond the scope of Christ's transforming Spirit." My point in quoting these texts is to demonstrate that Georgetown still speaks of itself as its first founders did, and it offers the Jesuit community an opportunity to help make real this ideal synthesis of human life and Christian culture which ought to give Georgetown its unique identity.

In claiming a role for the Jesuit community in working out the synthesis of Christianity and human culture to which Georgetown aspires, I have made much of the community's roots in the university's past. I should add that simply as a Catholic university, Georgetown has roots that go far deeper than the founding of the college in 1789. It derives its ideal of learning and virtue from a tradition of Christian humanism that began with the Fourth Gospel and the writings of St. Paul, and has continued through Augustine, Aquinas, Newman, Rahner, and Teilhard de Chardin, whose visionary words, so faithfully Pauline, are inscribed above the entrance to this hall. The truth is that no secular university can claim that tradition as anything but an option—an elective course. It is not the core of a secular institution's intellectual life as it is of Georgetown's.

Within the broad tradition of Christianity, certain subcultures have flourished in religious orders and contributed much to the general good. I think this is true of the Society of Jesus. Like the Benedictines, the Franciscans, the Dominicans, our order has its own special themes and insights, and through the instrumentality of the Jesuit community they have been added to Georgetown's treasure. Two years ago in a convocation address, Father Healy proposed to the faculty the characteristically Ignatian synthesis of contemplation and action as a pattern for the life of this university. For Ignatius, contemplation fulfills itself in action when and if it begins and ends with love.

This Ignatian theme was first enunciated in the sixteenth century. In our own day the Society of Jesus, following the lead of the universal church, has come to define its mission as the service of faith and the promotion of that justice which is an integral part of faith. Indeed, Jesuits today are asked to make faith and justice an overriding perspective of all their ministries. It's safe to say, because the Jesuit Superior General said it only recently, that Jesuits in higher education have struggled with this ideal with only mixed success, recognizing its validity and urgency in the modern world but wondering how it is to be applied in a university, whose immediate aim is not to evangelize or to reform society. The debate about this ideal has already taken place at Georgetown and its effects on the life of the university in this past decade can be observed. I would contend that Georgetown has been enriched because some of its Jesuit and lay members have placed this ideal insistently before the larger university community.

The Society of Jesus offers Georgetown themes and ideals to enrich the university's understanding of the Christian tradition. It can also offer a method with which to bring these essentially gospel ideals to bear on the living of one's life. I mean the Spiritual Exercises of St. Ignatius. They are by no means an arcane discipline intelligible only to Jesuits. The members of the Society ought to offer to share them with any member of the university community who is trying to discover how concretely to live out his or her commitment to God.

I've tried to show how Georgetown offers the Society of Jesus a unique challenge as an apostolic order. That challenge is a tension between opportunities and obstacles. Let me speak now of the obstacles. And let me begin with the Jesuit community.

This year fifty-seven of its members are active in the university—at least they tell me they are. Ten years from now seventeen of them, or thirty percent of the whole community, will have retired. I would expect that a few young Jesuits will be available to take their place, but certainly not seventeen. The replacements are simply not there. Last year three men entered the Maryland Province of the Society. This year there may be eight or nine.

Frankly, I don't think that we have to have fifty-seven Jesuits to maintain the mission of the Society at Georgetown. But we must have some men. They must be dedicated, and they must know how to maintain a balance between their inclination as priests and religious toward pastoral care and the commitment that every university member must make to the central task of the university: teaching at the highest level of intensity, learning and researching and sharing one's discoveries with the learned, not simply to get tenure, but because this is what makes a university the wondrous thing that it is. There are many ways in which Jesuits and non-Jesuits alike can contribute to the life and continued growth of Georgetown and to the purposes of the Society in this institution. But few are more important in the long run than research, scholarship and therefore teaching at the very highest level of one's discipline. It is the kind of service that Jesuits in the past have not given Georgetown often enough. Its scarcity in the future would seriously diminish the contributions that the Society can make to Georgetown's life as a university.

Let me speak of another obstacle that I see to the Jesuit mission here, though in naming it I realize I may reveal the Jansenism of my ancestors. The very success that Georgetown has enjoyed in recent years has its shadow side. A casual visitor to our campus will learn quickly enough that Georgetown has become a fashionable, perhaps even a glamorous place to be. Working with bright and agreeable young people in a fairly self-contained world is always a danger for their elders. The stated aim of the university is in some way to teach not only economics and chemistry but that Christian humanism which it professes. But our students are also powerful though unwitting teachers. They are instinctively in tune with the values of contemporary American culture, some of which stand in direct contradiction to Christianity. Sometimes I think that in distracted moments, some of us muse on Georgetown as a kind of Princeton on the Potomac. Such an institution would have little connection with the college that John Carroll founded.

Let me speak of one other obstacle that I see to the Jesuit mission at Georgetown. I mentioned earlier that one of the attractions of this place to the Society is that it offers an opportunity to propose to a university community the ideal of struggling for justice as a necessary consequence of professing Christian faith. But how is such an integration to be conceived and lived out in a university, which is oriented toward contemplation and learning, and whose purposes can easily be subverted by the intrusion of social and political activism? Georgetown, urged on, I am happy to say, by members of the Jesuit community, has had considerable success in encouraging its undergraduate students to deepen their understanding of human society as it really is through programs that bring them in contact with the poor. It has been less successful in exploring within the classroom and in its research the difficult region where social reality and moral principle intersect.

Recently, the Superior General of the Society, Father Peter-Hans Kolvenbach, addressed this precise issue when he spoke to the presidents of Jesuit universities around the world. Being a brave man, he tried to give an instance of what he meant. He told the presidents that "economics, for example, while it has its own methods and rules, when taught and studied from the perspective of the promotion of justice, will refuse to be locked into a concept of economy which only deals with 'things,' but will see that it has to consider the relationships among persons; in this perspective, economics will see material things as instruments for the service of individual people." I fear that some professors here would describe Father General's position, with all respect, as uninformed drivel.

Let me mention one last problem that I see before us. The ideal which Georgetown attempts is to be a community of scholars and learners committed to the pursuit of harmony between human knowledge and supernatural faith—*utraque unum.* The truth is that many members of the university's faculty have little interest in such a vision or anything like it.

They tend their own gardens admirably but see little connection between what they do and the professed purposes of the university. Surely, Georgetown is and must always remain an open institution. There is such a thing as healthy pluralism of views and it should certainly be found here. Still, it is difficult to see how this university can make any approach to its Catholic and Jesuit ideal unless its teachers are at least in sympathy with the institution's purposes. Which would bring me to the very delicate matter of hiring and tenure, if I were not polite and the evening already far spent.

In the Book of Deuteronomy Moses says to the people of Israel: "I have set before you life and death, the blessing and the curse. Choose life, then, that you and your descendants may live" (Dt 30:19). Despite the obstacles that it faces here, despite the weakness that it finds within itself, the Society of Jesus commits itself to the life of this place of Catholic learning, and in doing so renews its own life. The Jesuits' involvement in the life of Georgetown ought to be rich and varied. It should go beyond the classroom and the laboratory and the library to include the chapel and the residence hall. My own discussion of the Jesuits' role in the university has neglected the whole aspect of promoting Georgetown as a community not only of scholars and learners but also of human beings and friends, many of whom are drawn together around the Holy Eucharist. But if I were asked to single out for the Jesuit community one concrete task that would enhance the university's life, I would say it is the task of telling Georgetown and the world who Georgetown is. If the university is to be true to its past and its future, then it must rediscover itself constantly.

I have argued that the Jesuit community has a special role in this process of guarding and passing on the flame. But the Jesuits at Georgetown, though they have special reason to cherish and promote the idea of this university, can hardly be called the only keepers of the flame. That ideal and its cherishing is just as precious to the non-Jesuits here this evening as it is to the Jesuits. Your presence demonstrates your own desire to define Georgetown for the future, and, like Hamlet's friend, Horatio, to tell its story (5.2.349).

Georgetown is a challenge not only to the Society of Jesus but to all the men and women who are a part of it and love it. It offers all of us the opportunity to bring two things into harmony: the advancement of learning, and thus of our fellow human beings, and the greater glory of God. May all of us, Jesuit and lay, hear and respond to this challenge.

LEO J. O'DONOVAN, S.J.

Many Worlds and One World: Georgetown and the Society of Jesus in Their American Context

LEO J. O'DONOVAN, S.J., is Professor of Systematic Theology at the Weston School of Theology.

Georgetown, like any great university, belongs to the world. Reaching out toward human welfare in an unconditional way, its concerns transcend the particularities of its foundation, its geographical location, and the immediate interests of its various constituencies. And yet, again like any genuine university, Georgetown is rooted in its country and its culture, its religious context and catholicity. At these wells we draw life.

These are the themes I wish to explore with you tonight: how Georgetown belongs to the world and yet to many worlds, how it can be particular and yet have universal concerns. Paradoxically, we might even put the point this way: Can we really hope for one common world if we do not first recognize that we live in many particular worlds? In the five sections that follow I shall be considering with you first Georgetown's origin and the world it belongs to and then the many worlds it is called to encounter. In a third section I shall offer some guidelines for discovering what may be common to time's many worlds. After discussing the value of a contextual approach to cultural pluralism, I shall finally comment on our American context in particular and the role played in it by religion, American Catholicism and Catholic universities.

I. A World of Beginnings

We should not underestimate the coincidence of our country's foundation and Georgetown's. Those thirteen colonies with their three million inhabitants were a fragile but great experiment, a radical adventure in a new world that proved in the outcome to be remarkably hospitable to wave after wave of settlers, not least among them many Catholics. Estimates for the Catholic population in 1789 range from eighteen to thirty thousand. At the least, a very small minority was in question. Though many of them were poor, many were also strongly sympathetic to their country's principles of freedom and democracy. After being nominated by his fellow priests, John Carroll became the first archbishop of the Catholic Church in the United States. For two decades after the ratification of the Constitution, Catholics under his leadership participated quite openly in the developing life of their new nation.

In a memorandum he had prepared for Rome in 1786, Carroll wrote:

> In 1776, the American independence was declared, and a revolution effected, not only in political affairs but also in those relating to Religion. For while the thirteen provinces of North America rejected the yoke of England, they proclaimed at the same time, freedom of conscience, and the right of worshiping the Almighty, according to the spirit of the religion to which each one should belong . . . After the war . . . the good effects of freedom of conscience began to develop themselves.[1]

Thus, in accord with the "liberal principle of our Constitution," as Carroll called it, the proposal for establishing an academy at Georgetown announced that it would be "open to students of every religious profession.—They, who in this respect differ from the superintendents of the Academy, will be at Liberty to frequent the Places of Worship and Instruction appointed by their parents; but with respect to their moral conduct, all must be subject to general and uniform Discipline."[2] If the new nation offered freedom of conscience and religion to Catholics in search of truth, then it surely behooved them to be equally welcoming to all their fellow citizens.

Georgetown was thus a small but significant experiment within the larger experiment of a federal union that was born of a curiously conservative revolution. The young nation with its uncharted frontiers had many roots in the Old World but it was truly a new beginning. No one could know how far it would progress.

In somewhat analogous fashion, the Society of Jesus, from whose members came Georgetown's first planners, had also been established as an experiment and a new beginning. Formally founded in 1540 with the approbation of Pope Paul III, the Society's spiritual origins reached further back into the experience of Ignatius of Loyola which he recorded in manual fashion in his classic little book, the *Spiritual Exercises.* In the first lecture in this series, Brian Daley spoke eloquently of the three elements that characterize the movement of the *Spiritual Exercises:* wonder, freedom, and practical commitment. Over the years of his leadership in Rome, Ignatius was to incorporate those movements into the social and institutional expression of how his companions in the Lord would serve the glory of God and the welfare of humanity. During those years he wrote *The Constitutions of the Society of Jesus,* giving historical structure and embodiment to the practical elections for the kingdom of Christ that had been made by the first Jesuits.

The origin of the Jesuits had also its dimensions of the mystery of providence. And when the first American Jesuits turned to consider the establishment of an academy at Georgetown on the Potomac, their Society had in fact been suppressed for over a decade. Would it ever live again? Would the small institution with which John Carroll was concerned live on? Amazingly enough, commitment to the purposes and ideals both of the new nation and of the old religious order seems to have nourished intelligence and courage enough for them both eventually to flourish.

Those were the beginnings. In a genuinely new world, an expansion and adventurous new version of the old world began. Of course, a common concept of the world was presupposed at the time by ordinary citizens and thinkers alike. Politically, it derived from the deist form of enlightenment thought that characterized the great early figures of American history. Philosophically, it bore the imprint of a newly historical and scientific conception of reality. Biblically, it owed its shape in good measure to the creation account of the Hebrew Scriptures which saw a good world coming forth from the hands of the creator God. The narrative framework of salvation history was less prominent at that time, although the many stories of God's providence and action among God's people helped to sustain the notion that the people of the covenant made their way through time in God's one world.

Two centuries later, Christian theology still presupposes in a general way the concept of a unitary world. Karl Rahner, for example, argued that the world of spirit and matter is one in its origin, in its history, and in its goal.[3] Coming from the infinite, absolute and one reality of the holy mystery whom Christians call God, the world in Rahner's view should be seen as humanity's environment. It moves through history toward the fulfillment that will be constituted by final union with its creator and redeemer God. Writing at the time of the Second Vatican Council and in serious conversation with evolutionary thought, Rahner was concerned to affirm the integrity of the created order. Later, in fact, he gave more attention to the relativity of that order and its pluralistic character.[4] Both the logic of history and the experience of the church's renewal at the Council required this reconsideration, to which I shall later return.

But first I wish simply to imagine again our one world with its many promising and risky beginnings, the world to which this university belongs beyond its apparent and all too often real limitations of time and place and ambition. You and I live in a larger world than Washington, and as students and educators we must be reminded of the full horizon of the truth we seek at this university. In the late winter of 1987, I was vividly reminded of that vast horizon when I made my first trip to Asia. In the course of the journey of twenty-four days, we circled the world entirely in fewer days than it would have taken Ignatius Loyola to cross Europe to Rome, or John Adams to sail from Boston to Philadelphia, or Ben Franklin to cross the Atlantic. Returning home exhilarated, deeply moved, and fairly exhausted, I knew in body and soul how one our world is.

II. Many Worlds

But is it really one world? Geologically that may be the case, or at least geographically. In many ways, however, the historical experience of recent centuries, together with the new science and technology accompanying it, suggests that the map of our earth in fact encloses many worlds. Since the founding of the Society of Jesus in the sixteenth century and the founding of this university two centuries later, Western culture has passed through an age of discovery, an age of revolutions, an industrial age, and now the nuclear age. Not only down through time, but even now in our present, apparently homogeneous time, we can pass not simply through different experiences of the world but through radically different ways of being in the world. Since there is no truly human world apart from human culture, we must take seriously the evidences of differing language, art, religion, science and technology. Together they constitute cultures truly distinct from one another, perhaps not at odds with one another, but by no means necessarily in communication with one another either.

By this I do not mean to propose a relativism of culture. I do insist, however, that our experiences of history, of scientific relativity, and also of the many approaches to ultimate religious reality have brought home to us profound questions about the sense in which our world is one. If Georgetown belongs to the world, it is equally true to say that the university has many worlds to meet. Pluralism is not an accidental aspect of our situation. It is of the essence.[5]

Over the last twenty-five years, this situation has been focused in inescapably new ways for American Catholics too. Let me indicate very briefly four dimensions of how radically we now experience pluralism.

First, I think it is true to say that through the upheaval of the Vietnam War and through exposure to the revolutions of 1968, American society has entered a significantly new phase of its history. No longer the promising innocent nation, no longer the dominant imperial power, no longer the assured pragmatic adventure, the United States suddenly sees itself no longer at the center of the world. We have become one shaper, among many, of different possible worlds. And our awareness of our national identity has begun to admit a corresponding new sense of ambiguity.

In this bicentennial year of the United States Constitution, there are signs that we have begun to read the Constitution accordingly. Are President Reagan and former Chief Justice Warren Burger, in the company of many other traditional interpreters, really correct in saying that the Constitution guaranteed liberty for all Americans from the moment it was composed in Philadelphia in 1787? I do not mean to slight the founders of the nation, nor the remarkable achievement of the most enduring national polity presently existent. Our Constitution was framed with extraordinary wisdom and flexibility. But it is also true that two centuries ago many Americans were *not* yet included within the full scope of that Constitution. It took decades for many of them, black and white, men and women, to secure their rights under the Constitution. Without the abolitionists, the civil rights movement, and women's movements, "life, liberty and the pursuit of happiness" would be far more restricted than proud Americans today imagine. One may well say with Justice Felix Frankfurter that the Constitution, rather than being a fixed and final text, was "most significantly not a document but a stream of history."[6] It was an unfinished work in an unfinished world. Or in one world among many.

A second line of evidence may be taken from the Roman Catholic Church's experience of renewal or aggiornamento at the Second Vatican Council. Seeing the church as a mystery of witness to God's purposes of love in our world, the Council reconceived the world as a place of mission awaiting the dawning of "a new heaven and a new earth."[7] Called out of its defensive, self-enclosed posture, the church saw itself summoned to join the common pilgrimage of humanity in search of its ultimate destiny. It came even to speak of many churches. And considering its recognition of how unfinished the world is, we may say that it suggested by implication that there are many worlds in which human beings live and have lived.

David Tracy has interpreted the situation boldly and comments: "It is quite clear that Catholicism is going through the greatest change since its passage from a Jewish sect to a Greco-Roman religion. The ways of being

Catholic will necessarily multiply and the church will be more diverse; pluralism in religious expression will increase, not decrease."[8] We do not have, in other words, an objectively fixed world in which Catholic faith may simply serve as leaven or light for transformation. Different patterns of experience and worlds of expectation meet each other even within the same continent, and often seem to clash irrevocably. We recognize with pain the increasing difficulty of dialogue between different continents and, perhaps most of all, between our northern and southern hemispheres. Neither the speed of travel and communication nor the technological possibility of a global village should blind us to the fact that on our apparently unitary planet human beings today live at different historical times and in different cultural worlds.

If American society and the Catholic Church face radically new periods in their history, and indeed new worlds, much the same may be said, but of course more modestly, for the Society of Jesus. Since its foundation, the Company of Jesus has been called to seek and to encounter the different world cultures in order to bring the gospel to them. Just imagine Francis Xavier travelling to Goa, Robert DeNobili to India, Mateo Ricci to China. Centuries later, John Courtney Murray was another kind of explorer, venturing to explain a new world of relations between church and secularized state. These are just a few examples that suggest the inner missionary core of a Jesuit vocation. It is a vocation that seeks to remain faithful to its original charism but also truly to incarnate it in the many worlds to which Jesuits are sent in the course of time.

"In this 'new age' in which the human race now finds itself," decreed the thirty-first General Congregation in 1965,

> the Society of Jesus, according to the spirit of the whole Church, which is itself in process of renewal, recognizes the difficulties with regard to its goal and plan of life which are arising from the changes that have taken place in humanity's way of living and thinking. At the same time it recognizes the opportunities which arise from the new developments in our world and those which flow from the renewal of the Church that has been begun by the Council. It intends, therefore, to take a very close look at its own nature and mission in order that, faithful to its own vocation, it can renew itself and adapt its life and its activities to the exigencies of the Church and the needs of contemporary humanity.[9]

For an incisive commentary on the thirty-first General Congregation and on the thirty-second General Congregation that followed it ten years later, I recall the last homily that Father Pedro Arrupe gave on July 31, 1981, at the Ateneo de Manila. Father Arrupe spoke there of "the reformulation of the purpose of the Society; from 'the defense and propagation of the faith' to 'the service of the faith and promotion of justice.' The new formulation is in no way reductive, deviationist or disjunctive," he said; "rather it brings out elements germinally contained in the old formulation, through a more explicit reference to the present needs of the Church and of humanity to whose service (Jesuits) are committed by (their) vocation."[10]

Father Arrupe also spoke of the *Constitutions* as

> an unfinished text which, under the illumination of the Spirit, is constantly filled out in the course of history, developing its latent and fundamental thrusts which are contained in the Exercises. . . . Historical continuity in cultural diversity is precisely the guarantee of legitimacy. That is why the Society today, living and working in different and rapidly changing circumstances, has had to change much if it is to preserve its "Ignatianess," to be faithful to its foundational and institutional charism, and yet hold on to the unchanging essentials.[11]

These are probing comments, I think—incomplete perhaps, but rich in interpretation and suggestion.

If the experience of many worlds has so affected American society, the Catholic Church and the Society of Jesus, we may then ask more briefly: What about Georgetown? Well, I was a student here even before the shifts of the sixties. Now when I look about at the Medical Center, at the burgeoning main campus, at the national prominence of the Law School, at the quality of students and faculty, when I consider the university's reputation growing apace with its endowment and, yes, also our great successes on the basketball courts, well, it's still my Alma Mater, and yet it is clearly also a *new* Georgetown.

III. Lear's Question

Up until now I have been contrasting our experience of an apparently unitary world with the many worlds of more exact historical and cultural experience. From various perspectives, American, Catholic, Jesuit, I have tried to discover the complexity beneath our often naive first impression of reality. But what prevents the picture I have drawn from being purely relativistic—or perhaps a merely verbal paradox? What actual or possible continuity, what emerging identity may there be between the many worlds of our late twentieth century and a common world germinally present or promised perhaps in them all? Earlier in this series, Father James Devereux recalled for you King Lear's question: "Who is it that can tell me who I am?"[12] The many worlds of human experience pose their own version of that question.

Principles of identity and continuity are surely not the same for individuals and societies, much less for worlds. But there do seem to be analogies between individuals and societies, at least to a limited extent, and analogous principles for their identity. These seem to me important not only for our understanding of the world but for our understanding of this university. Let me propose five for your consideration.[13]

In the first place, I suggest that we must always search for universality from a particular standpoint, that we may best work for a common world by truly inhabiting our own. In many ways this is a contemporary expression of the ancient philosophical problem of the one and the many, of unity in diversity. But as modern Western culture has become more aware of its historical conditioning and relativity, we see more clearly the need to approach our own world and other possible worlds not simply with a priori principles but rather with an openness to new insights and fresh principles that are generated by actual experience. In the late twentieth century, for example, our memory of the Holocaust has given us an almost mortally wounded sense of evil, while the discovery of nuclear power has posed us with a radically new responsibility for the care of our planet. The particularities of our world may well have deeper connections with other worlds than we realize. But we are likely to find those bonds realistically only by truly inhabiting our particular world and recognizing our responsibilities in it.

Will you excuse a theologian a theological example? (I am sure you're looking for something concrete.) Well, I recall the notion of the local church which was recovered at Vatican II. For the Council, the church of Christ is not in the first place a universal entity above time. It is rather a communion of local churches, in each of which the body of Christ and his Spirit are truly present. By truly belonging to one's own local church, in other words, one participates more authentically in the universal church.[14]

Second, in a pluralistic culture amid a plurality of worlds, we need to remain self-critical. Pluralism should not be accepted simply as a matter of fact. The more we come to understand, for example, the origins and development of our American pluralism, the better we may hope to guide its future. A "new pluralism" should also recognize more profoundly that it is dependent on various levels of personal association. Existing at different levels, through the voluntary association typical of American political parties, educational institutions and charitable organizations, it will only survive, as Martin Marty has argued, through generating a comunity of communities.[15] Such a pluralism must be genuinely hospitable, marked by real exchange between its constituents; its sense of community must cut the tangled roots of racism, sexism and religious discrimination that have previously choked its communal growth. A renewed pluralism, further, will require more public discussion. We have learned only slowly that history offers multiple perspectives on truth and not some timeless possession of it. In that case, different perspectives and world views need all the more to be in permanent, vigorous and open discussion. In sum, without serious self-criticism our American society today risks allowing its pluralistic heritage to degenerate into random diversity and relativism.

If I were to offer another theological example, it would be the recovered sense of the church's constant need for reformation. According to this principle, Christ's gathered community stands always in need of being renewed and reformed, in head and members. In no one of its churches can conversion for the sake of the Kingdom be taken for granted. In fact, where the church is most itself, there it is most aware of its own insufficiency and total dependence on its redeeming Creator.

As a third principle of continuity and identity, I suggest that we must recognize identity as cumulative through time, open and unresolved, rather than a permanent synthesis. Identity is subject to decline, just as it is born ultimately by God's judgment. Cultural identity, like psychological identity, cannot be satisfactorily construed in essentialist terms, supposing a core reality which simply endures through accidental change. In the American Civil War, for example, the very nature of a federal Union was at issue. But neither, on the other hand, can identity be properly understood as pure process, without a central, enduring meaning and purpose. As president, Abraham Lincoln drew his inspiration from a constructive reading of the Constitution. As a society enacts its identity in time, its members have reason to hope that they are indeed enacting themselves and forming a culture they may call their own.

A religious analogy? I would suggest the notion of the people of God as pilgrims, under way to their true home while making God's creation meanwhile as habitable as possible. Neither the church nor its members belong to Christ all at once. Led by his Spirit and sustained by his grace, they travel and toil up the steep, undivided road of faith and justice.[16]

Fourth, one may perhaps say that conversation is the most basic principle for all identity, conversation with one's self, with others, across cultures. We all know how easy it is to interpret ourselves only as others see us, neglecting to address and listen to our inner selves. We know how quickly we often pass by the real expression and intention even of our friends. Traveling abroad, many of us have had the unfortunate experience of the ugly American not only among the tourists in the bus but in our own oblivious selves. The "failures" of genuine conversation are all too frequent.

But if we suppose that conversation is possible, a give and take not simply about disparate selves but about the common subject of their views and ways of being in the world, if we suppose that human beings are always at least able to turn to one another and exchange their experience of their worlds, then perhaps we have real reason to hope that a common experience of a common world will arise. It may be that simple attention to one another must precede such real exchange, that mere presence must precede explicit dialogue. I suspect that imagination and a sense of playful interaction are more important than we have thought when we talk about interpersonal as well as intercultural dialogue. But it is clear at least that without dialogue in our rapidly changing worlds, they are all too likely to change in directions away from or even contrary to each other.

As a religious example of true con-verse, I suggest the central biblical notion of conversion. From the great prophets of Israel to the preaching of Jesus there is scarcely a more fundamental theme than the call to turn back, to face again the one true God. In doing so, Jews and Christians alike have their best hope of turning to one other.

In summary, I would say that it is of the essence of historical, linguistic reality to change in order to be itself. The worlds of our society and our church and our university, the other worlds of other societies and religions and schools, can only hope to be themselves and be in contact with one another by entering fully into the historical process. I believe this is true of our American constitutional experience. It seems to be an explicit theme of Catholicism still in the midst of a great process of renewal. We have seen Father Arrupe speak of the Society of Jesus in its necessary reformulation of purpose. In their differing ways, then, both individuals and societies can remain themselves only if they are willing to change in communication with others and in view of a greater common good.

Biblically as well, the good world sprung from the Creator's hands can only truly be itself if it is redeemed through a servant of God suffering for his people. The creation does not simply unfold toward its goal; it must above all be enfolded in God's saving love.

Let me turn now to some theoretical options that are available for seeing our world in conversation and in context.

IV. Worlds of Context

If we are to become present to the many worlds of human experience, then we must be present to our own. There is a risk, but an equal opportunity. Over the last twenty-five years, various watchwords have offered themselves for our guidance. One was the very notion of *pluralism,* but often presented as a characterization merely of different styles or ways of life within a single culture. In this essay I have tried to speak of our need for a renewed pluralism in the United States. Another key that offered itself was the notion of *the modern human being* experiencing the world not so much as ready-made but rather as material at hand for human fabrication. *Secularization* was yet another theme interpreting the world as come of age and calling us each to autonomous responsibility in it, with freedom from antiquated mythologies. Still another perspective was offered by the idea of a *counterculture,* setting itself in critical opposition to the mindless consumerism and other-directed conformism of a self-indulgent society.

More recently, a number of critics have emphasized the importance of social context for appreciating both one's standpoint in culture and the standpoints of other possible partners in dialogue. They suggest that we understand ourselves in proportion to our grasp of the artistic, religious, economic and political patterns and structures that crisscross to form our culture. Overcoming the notion of a transtemporal culture or an eternal world, focusing on historical rather than perennial truth, accepting the constant interplay of subjectivity and objectivity, a contextual mode of thought seeks as much understanding as is possible in the circumstances of actual life and allows the demand for certitude to retreat to its proper, very limited place in human affairs.

In religious thought, Robert Schreiter has recently distinguished three models typically used in reflecting theologically on social context. The first is a *translation model,* which proceeds in two steps. "In the first step, one frees the Christian message as much as possible from its previous cultural accretions. In so doing, the data of revelation are allowed to stand freely and be prepared for the second step of the procedure, namely, the translation into a new situation."[17] A guiding image for such an approach is that of the kernel and the husk, with the attempt being made to strip away the husk while preserving the kernel. Examples of the model are common from Adolf Harnack to Leslie Dewart calling for the de-hellenization of Western Christianity. Roman Catholics have largely followed this model in their liturgical renewal, and so have many Protestants in their efforts to find dynamic equivalents for basic biblical imagery and then to translate them into local languages. Commonly, the translation model suffers two major weaknesses, one a positivist understanding of culture, another the supposition that biblical revelation or church teaching can occur in a privileged, supracultural sphere.

A second model may be called the *adaptation model.* It seeks a more basic encounter between Christianity and culture. One version of it relies on philosophical models from the West as a guide to develop an explicit philosophy or world view from within another culture. Another version uses the Reformation concepts of the New Testament church as its paradigm and tries to understand a sister church in a new culture as an instance of it. Still a third version was embodied in Pope Paul VI's address to the African bishops in Kampala, Uganda in 1969. There the pope said:

> The expression, that is, the language and mode of manifesting this one Faith, may be manifold; hence, it may be original, suited to the tongue, the style, the genius, and the culture, of the one who professes this one Faith. From this point of view, a certain pluralism is not only legitimate, but desirable. An adaptation of the Christian life in the fields of pastoral, ritual, didactic and spiritual activities is not only possible, it is even favored by the Church. The liturgical renewal is a living example of this. And in this sense you may, and you must, have an African Christianity.[18]

Schreiter discusses a third set of models that stand in close relation to the adaptation models but consider more specifically the cultural context in which Christianity develops and seeks its appropriate expression. These models *begin* their reflection with the cultural context and may be called *contextual* in a strict sense. They recognize that almost all cultures are in the process of continual social change. In many areas of the world, however, this change is not only rapid but oppressive and dehumanizing. Depending on which of these basic social factors is emphasized, contextual thought takes one of two basic directions. If it is concerned primarily with cultural identity, it is generally called an ethnographic approach. If it concentrates on oppression and social ills and thus on the need for social change, it is typically called a liberation approach.

Most basically, the difference between the contextual model and the adaptation model is that a local contextual theology "begins with the needs of a people in a concrete place, and from there moves to the traditions of faith."[19] The ethnographic approach may often be more a project than an accomplishment. It may easily overlook conflictual factors within a culture. It may fall prey to culture romanticism. But it rightly recognizes that a true conversation between gospel traditions and local cultural traditions is possible in principle and indeed of great importance. Rather than being concerned with issues of identity and continuity, on the other hand, liberation models concentrate on social change and discontinuity. They begin from the experience of widespread poverty, violence, and the denial of human rights. The outrage engendered by these experiences may diminish attention to the full biblical witness or induce uncritical enthusiasm for certain tools of social analysis. But those possible shortcomings cannot belie the power of liberation theologies and their capacity to speak the actual language of Christian communities.

As Americans, of course, we have not been studied extensively from either the ethnographic or the liberationist perspective.[20] But a sense of our real context is nevertheless vital for us too, if we are to live realistically in our own world and hope to communicate with others. In the last section of this essay, I want to reflect with you on that context.

V. The American Context

Our context both as Americans and as Catholics, I believe, is clearly at a point of crisis. We face changes more rapid than we can understand or control. But let us at least try to understand where we are.

First, gathering at a Christian university, I think it is important to recognize that as a nation we are far more religious than we have recently been encouraged to believe. In an ironic way, Martin Marty points to this fact merely by the titles of two of his books. In one he called us *A Nation of Believers.* In another he warned us that we too easily style ourselves *The Righteous Empire.*

Harvard, celebrating its 350th anniversary earlier this year, took the occasion to reevaluate the religious significance of its foundation. In 1936, Samuel Eliot Morison, writing the tercentennial history of the university, argued that Harvard's founders, scores of whom had graduated from Oxford or Cambridge, were dedicated to a recognizably secular liberal education. But now, 350 years after the foundation, prominent members of the history department at Harvard argue that the founders wanted specifically to build a Puritan college differing radically from the religiously corrupt old schools of Europe. They dreaded that the new colony might slip backward and that its ministers might grow ignorant. *Veritas* in Harvard's motto meant for them "God's truth." According to Bernard Bailyn, it was an intensely religious and ascetic Puritan culture that created the institution and carried it through precarious years into the stability of the eighteenth century.

Second, the role of American Catholics in the American context has changed notably. In a book just published, George Gallup, Jr. and Jim Castelli offer significant evidence on the beliefs, practices and values of the American Catholic people today. They indicate that American Catholics no longer worry about their acceptance in the larger society. They are concerned instead about how to lead. Since John Kennedy's presidency, they have acquired amazing new influence economically, socially, politically, and spiritually. Leaders of the church both here and abroad should reflect carefully on the impact Catholics may have on American society over the next twenty-five years.

Gallup and Castelli believe there are five major negative stereotypes about American Catholics that are held by church leaders as well as by ordinary members of the church. They argue that these stereotypes can be easily refuted. Contrary to the view that religious activity is declining among Catholics, the authors hold that stability and growth more accurately characterize Catholic religious life today. Contrary to the stereotype that young Catholics are leaving the church, they say that many indeed leave for a time but only to return with more serious purpose.

Contrary to the thesis that higher education is a sign of likely disaffection from the church, they say:

> The truth is that college-educated Catholics are the cutting edge of the Church, more involved in the Church and more satisfied by their involvement: 61% of college graduates and 55% of those with some college attend Mass in a given week; Catholics with a college background are no less likely to be involved in religious practices than Catholics with less education; 60% of those with a college background rate the Church as "excellent" or "good" in meeting their needs.[21]

Contrary further to the stereotype that Catholic women are in a state of revolt, the authors respond that "Catholic women do want much more from their Church, but they have not given up their belief that it is still *their* Church."[22] Finally, against the view that affluence has diminished Catholic interest in issues of justice and peace, Gallup and Castelli discover that "among Catholics, 84% supported bilateral nuclear freeze, 77% increased government spending on social spending, 69% supported the Equal Rights Amendment, and 68% want to cut military spending; on these issues and many others, Catholics are more liberal than the general population and are clearly in the liberal camp."[23]

While *The American Catholic People* rejects certain mistaken generalizations, it does take notice of two serious problems, and surprising ones at that. One is the question of how a newly middle-class church can continue to serve Catholics who are not in that mold. With its traditional emphasis on family life and its origins among the poor and immigrants, Catholicism must develop a new way to welcome the unmarried and the new immigrants. "There is a real danger of the Church becoming polarized, containing an increasingly affluent white middle-class and a struggling minority class who are strangers to one another."[24]

A second issue has to do with the church's participation in social and political matters. Apparently, a majority of Catholics agree with their bishops' positions on questions such as arms control, Central America, abortion, education and economic policy. Yet there is still a strong resistance to the church's involvement in the political sphere. Gallup and Castelli interpret this as a need for a stronger rationale for what the bishops say about public questions. They also feel that the bishops have not satisfactorily convinced Catholics at large that the bishops are acting in a well-informed and clearly nonpartisan way.

Gallup and Castelli conclude their informative study by some reflections on "the Catholicization of American culture." They feel that Catholics have made a special contribution to America precisely in those areas where they differ somehow from American Protestants. In fact, in many cases Catholics have been the leaders in these matters, taking a direction in which they were later joined by Protestants. They single out five issues.

1. Catholics typically show greater tolerance for diversity in religion, race and life style.
2. Catholics have strongly supported the promotion of women's rights in society at large.
3. Supported by their communal vision of society, Catholics have consistently urged government responsibility in meeting the needs of fellow Americans.
4. In presidential politics, Catholics have been the most important single group to swing a vote one way or another.
5. Without being strictly speaking pacifists, American Catholics have come to represent a strong commitment to world peace.

In these five aspects of the Catholicization of American culture, Gallup and Castelli see a movement

> toward a greater sensitivity to equality, justice, and peace, building upon the values of individual freedom and participatory democracy that were a legacy left by Evangelical and mainline Protestants who shaped the early days of the United States. That is no small achievement, and it is time that the American Catholic people are given their proper recognition for smoothing over some of the rough edges in the "Protestant nation" they came to as immigrants.[25]

What of the university's role in Catholicism's unique contribution to American society? Your own president, Father Timothy Healy, has eloquently expressed the role of a Catholic university in this situation. In the annual report for the year ended June 30, 1986, he suggested that if we put together two great insights, the autonomy of human culture and its explicit expression in universities that depend in some way or other on the church, "we find the exact dimensions and directions in which Catholic higher education in the United States has grown. . . . A Catholic university is different from American secular universities," he wrote,

> even though many of the latter were once religious foundations. In the Catholic university, by tradition and option, faith is part of the atmosphere. The church enjoys within the Catholic university the fullness of its sacramental life and the presence of ministers of that life. All Catholic universities teach Catholic theology as a serious intellectual discipline. One third element may be added. In Catholic universities, as both symbol of welcome to Catholic thought and indeed one of the principal instruments of its teaching, there is present a body of religious men or women, usually from the order responsible for the foundation of the university.[26]

At Georgetown, in particular, as Father Ronald Murphy explained in his lecture on the motto of the university's seal, *Utraque Unum,* the founders and their successors sought to foster a concourse, a lasting conversation if you will, between learning and virtue, between rational knowledge and evangelical faith, between secular culture and Christian vision, between the human and the divine.[27] My own favorite Georgetown expression of the university's aim, in fact, is emblazoned on the wall behind the stage of Gaston Hall, where one reads that marvelous paraphrase of the purpose of the Society of Jesus: *Ad Majorem Dei Gloriam inque salutem hominum* . . . "for the greater glory of God and the salvation, the welfare of human beings."

VI. In Conclusion

I conclude by reflecting briefly on our hope for a world to come. Throughout this presentation, I have been speaking of contributions made by the university, the church, and my own Society of Jesus in our human efforts to recognize the many worlds in which we live and the common world we might together come to inhabit. I see the university as a place of education for a world, the preparation of citizens, the cultivation of men and women who may become, in Wilfrid Desan's lovely expression, "planetary people." The church I understand as a community of witness, praise and service in the world. The Society of Jesus is a particular community serving both church and education, joining them to foster worlds in conversation, with the hope of one world.

I wanted to suggest that a common world is indeed more our hope than our realized situation. It seems to me not only realistic but greatly beneficial to recognize the many worlds in which human beings live, the particularities and limitations of our own world, but also the grounded possibility and divine guarantee that a single world is possible. Indeed, for Hebrew and Christian Scripture, there is a world to come for which all great hearts hope. The Hebrew prophets speak of a day of God that will be a day of wrath but still more of justice. Jesus proclaims the coming and already inaugurated kingdom of his Father. All Christian churches long and labor for that kingdom of justice and peace where Christ will reign forever. The Spirit of God is the guarantee poured daily into our hearts that this hope against all hope will not be confounded.

On the one hand, we may take solace from our current situation of crisis that old and backward ways are being sloughed off in our culture and in our church. We may look for promising beginnings, fresh approaches to questions old and new, the vitalization of our culture and community through the influx of new people from the southern hemisphere and from southeast Asia. In short, we may rightly feel ourselves called to courage in this crisis, looking upon it as a time neither of disaster nor of decline but rather as a decisive turning point in our history. We may regard it as a moment of opportunity for the great democratic revolution of equality which Alexis de Tocqueville called "the most uniform, the most ancient, and the most permanent tendency that is to be found in history."[28]

On the other hand, we must be Christian realists. The outcome of courage and the fulfillment of our lives do not lie entirely within the scope of our own forces. They depend ultimately upon God's grace. I have seen this in vivid form most recently as a brave young Jesuit friend of mine struggles against leukemia in a hospital on the other side of this nation. Gifted and generous, with a grand ability for music and for good stories, he seeks God's will in the midst of his leukemia, asking not simply that his health be restored but that God's love be proven. You can imagine how much I count on the great technical skill of the Fred Hutchison Cancer Center. And with what fervor I beg the Lord for Joe's cure. And ask for your prayers as well. But I cannot slack behind him in his willingness to accept any way in which God's glory may be shown. "For I am sure that neither death, nor life, nor angels, nor principalities, nor things present, nor things to come, nor powers, nor height, nor depth, nor anything else in all creation, will be able to separate us from the love of God in Christ Jesus our Lord" (Rom 8.38). Not from our world alone, and surely not from our current American context, even in its most generous openness toward forging a common human world, not from any of our works but only from the cross of Jesus Christ do we really have hope for God's true world to come.

Notes

1. Quoted in Georgetown University, Annual Report (30 June 1986), 1.

2. See John M. Daley, S.J., *Georgetown University: Origin and Early Years* (Washington, D.C., 1957) and Joseph T. Durkin, S.J., *Georgetown University: First In the Nation's Capital* (Washington, D.C.: Georgetown University Press, 1964).

3. "The Unity of Spirit and Matter in the Christian Understanding of Faith," *Theological Investigations* 6 (Baltimore: Helicon Press, 1969), 153-77.

4. Cf. L.J. O'Donovan, S.J., "A Journey into Time: The Legacy of Karl Rahner's Last Years," *Theological Studies* 46 (1985): 621-46.

5. See, for example, Leroy S. Rouner, ed., *Religious Pluralism* (Notre Dame, Indiana: University of Notre Dame Press, 1984).

6. As quoted in *The New York Times* in a discussion of the Bicentennial Celebration of the Constitution, 6 April 1987, A2.

7. Cf. 2 Cor 5:2; 2 Pt 3:13; *Gaudium et Spes* (Vatican Council II, *Pastoral Constitution on the Church in the Modern World*), art. 39.

8. Quoted in Eugene Kennedy, "A Dissenting Voice: The Creative Mind of Catholic Theologian, David Tracy," *The New York Times Magazine,* 9 November 1986, 30. For a more extended discussion, see Tracy's *Plurality and Ambiguity: Hermeneutics, Religion, Hope* (San Francisco: Harper & Row, 1987).

9. 31st General Congregation, decree 1, no. 1, in J.W. Padberg, S.J., ed., *Documents of the 31st and 32nd General Congregations of the Society of Jesus* (St. Louis: Institute of Jesuit Sources, 1977).

10. "Homily on the Feast of St. Ignatius," in *Leadership for Service* (Manila: Cardinal Bea Institute, 1983), 40-49, at 45.

11. Ibid., 44.

12. See Father Devereux's essay in this volume.

13. Such principles should not be merely physicalist. It is insufficient to describe a person, a culture or a world merely as a physical object operating according to material laws. Further, such principles cannot be merely extrinsic. They cannot impose an order or unity from without, whether by God's intention or human construction. Finally, the principles should not be objectivist, stating merely how things as a matter of fact are. To be human, our view of the world must be objective and yet not reduce it to a mere object. On the other hand, we should avoid principles which are merely spiritual, or intrinsic, or subjective. I try to avoid any of these extremes.

14. Cf. Avery Dulles, *The Catholicity of the Church* (Oxford: Clarendon Press, 1987).

15. Cf. Martin E. Marty, *The Public Church. Mainline—Evangelical—Catholic* (New York: Crossroad, 1981).

16. Cf. "Jesuits Today," no. 8, in J.W. Padberg, S.J., op.cit.

17. Robert J. Schreiter, *Constructing Local Theologies* (Maryknoll, N.Y.: Orbis Books, 1985), 7.

18. Cited in Schreiter, 11.

19. Ibid., 13.

20. Nevertheless, serious liberation literature is currently being developed by Blacks, Native Americans, women, and sexual minorities.

21. George Gallup, Jr., and Jim Castelli, *The American Catholic People. Their Beliefs, Practices and Values* (Garden City, N.Y.: Doubleday, 1987), 180.

22. Loc. cit.

23. Ibid., 181.

24. Ibid., 184.

25. Ibid., 191.

26. Georgetown University, Annual Report, June 30, 1986, 3-5.

27. See Father Murphy's essay in this volume.

28. Alexis De Tocqueville, *Democracy in America,* Phillips Bradley, ed. (New York: Knopf, 1966), vol. I, 3.